A Potpourri of Pictures

A Color Therapy Coloring Book

By

Kim Jordan Blair

I would like to thank my good friend Mary Ann Morrongiello Manders for coloring the giraffe and flowers picture on the cover of this book. I would also like to thank her for helping me choose the Title of this coloring book.

I also want to thank my dear friend Diane C. Holmes for coloring the fairy house under the wine glass picture on the cover of this book.

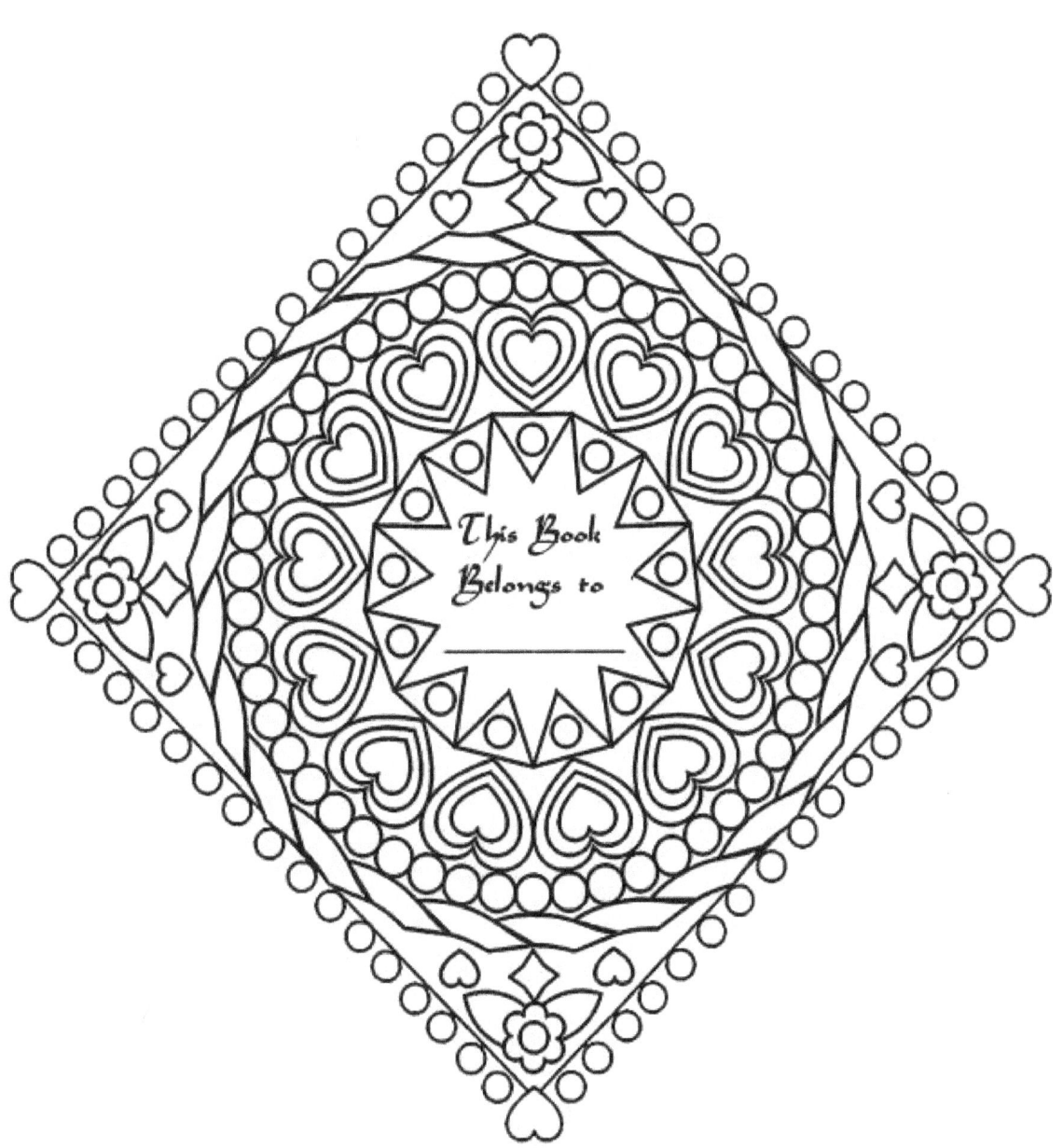

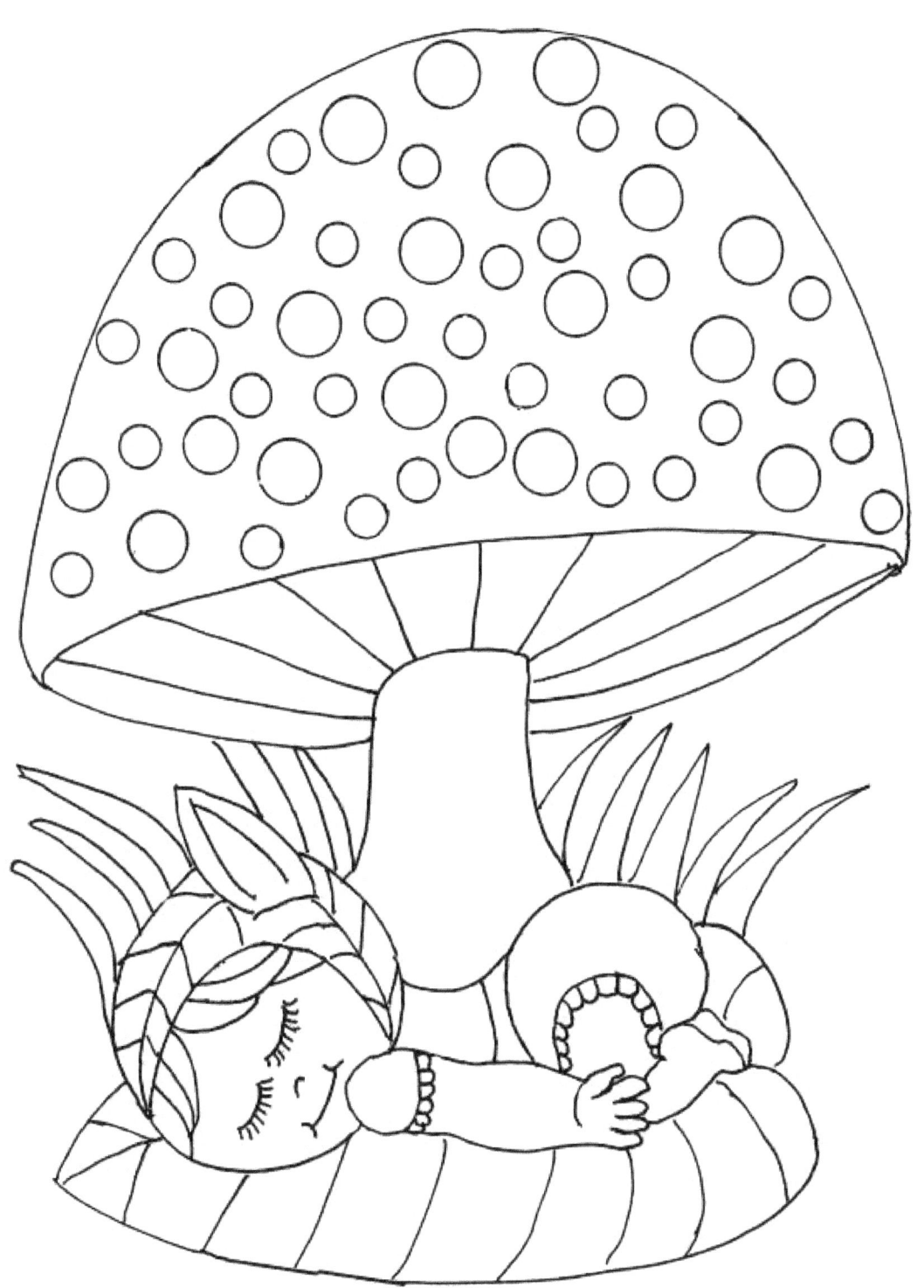

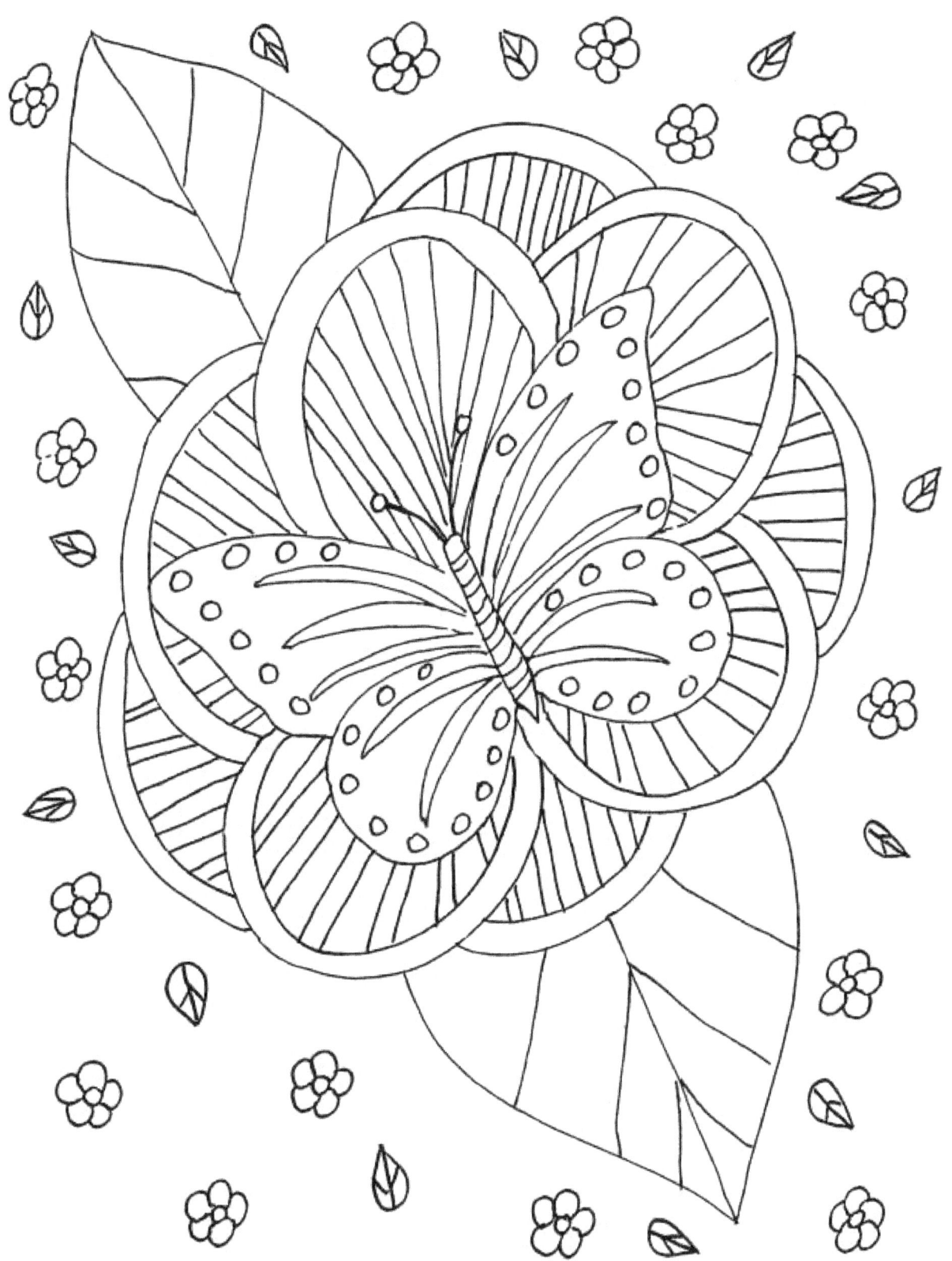

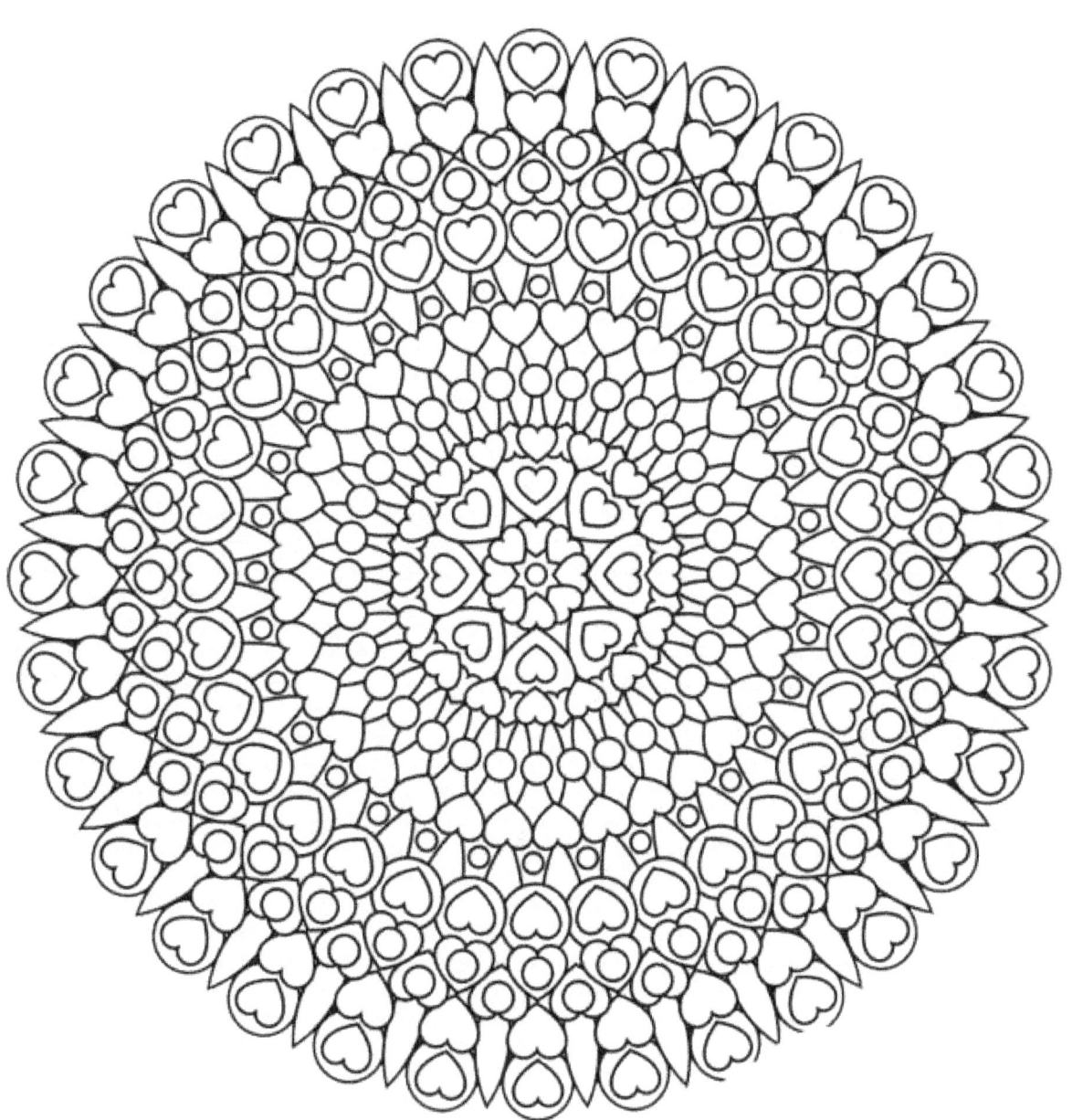

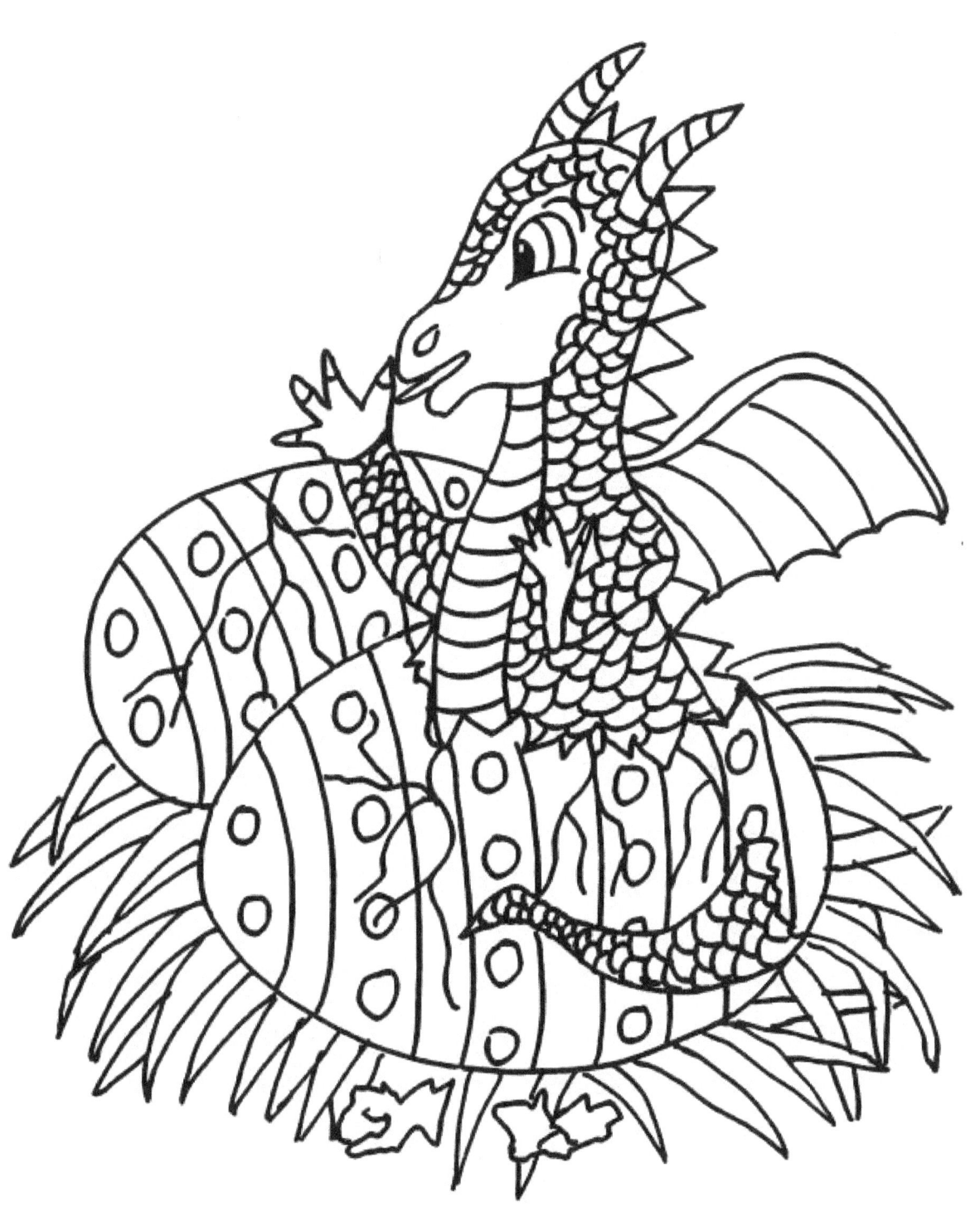

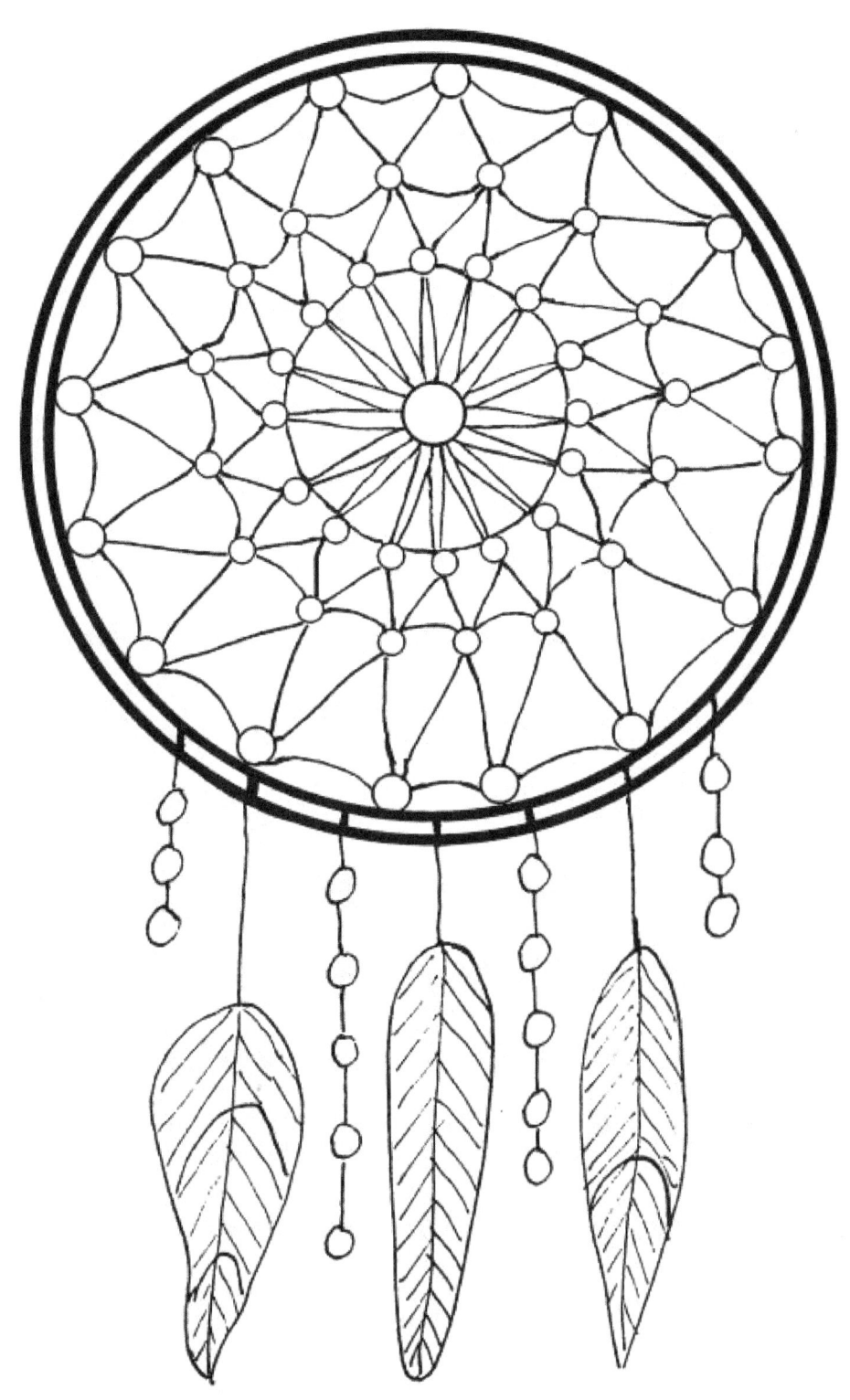

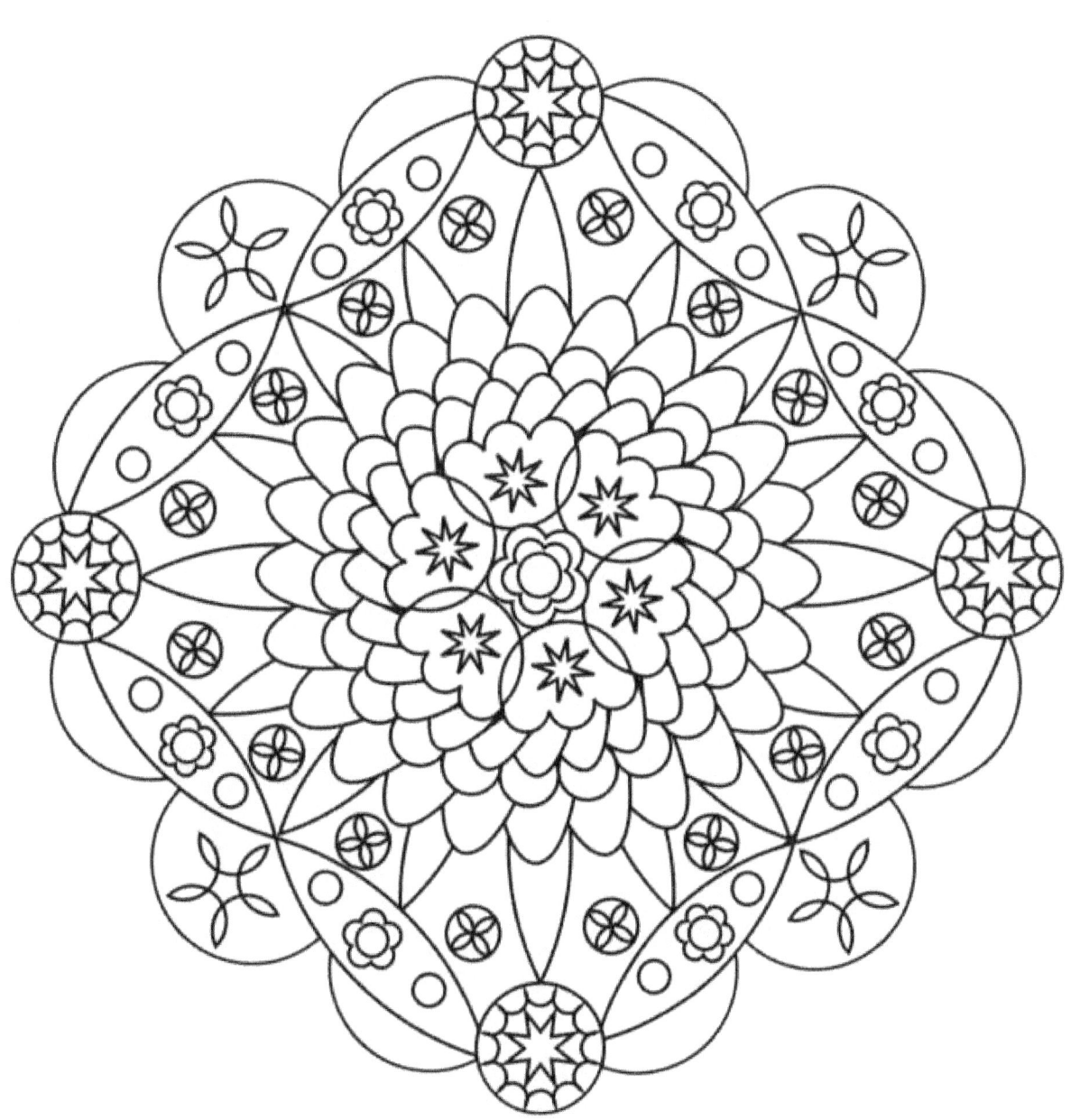

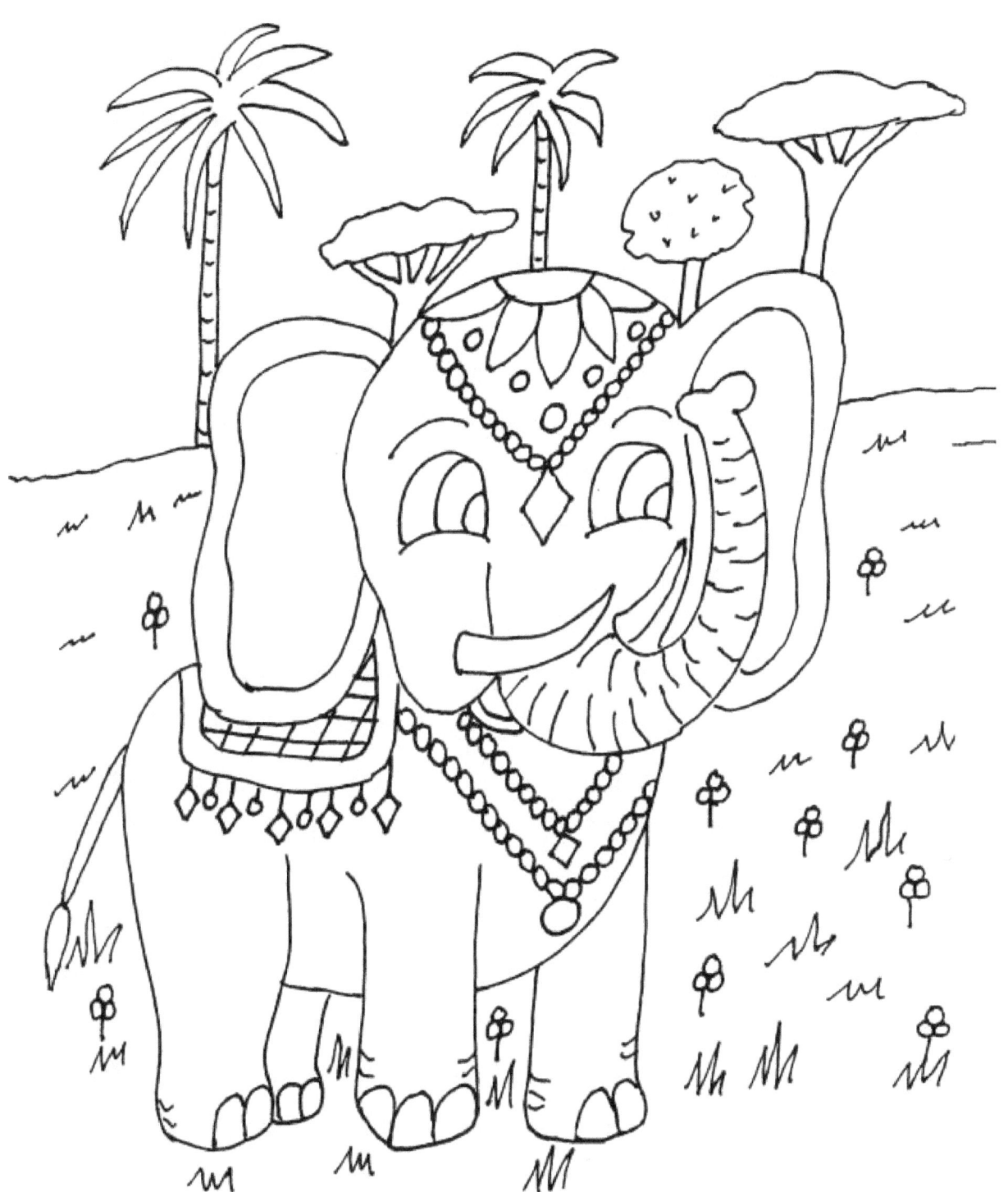

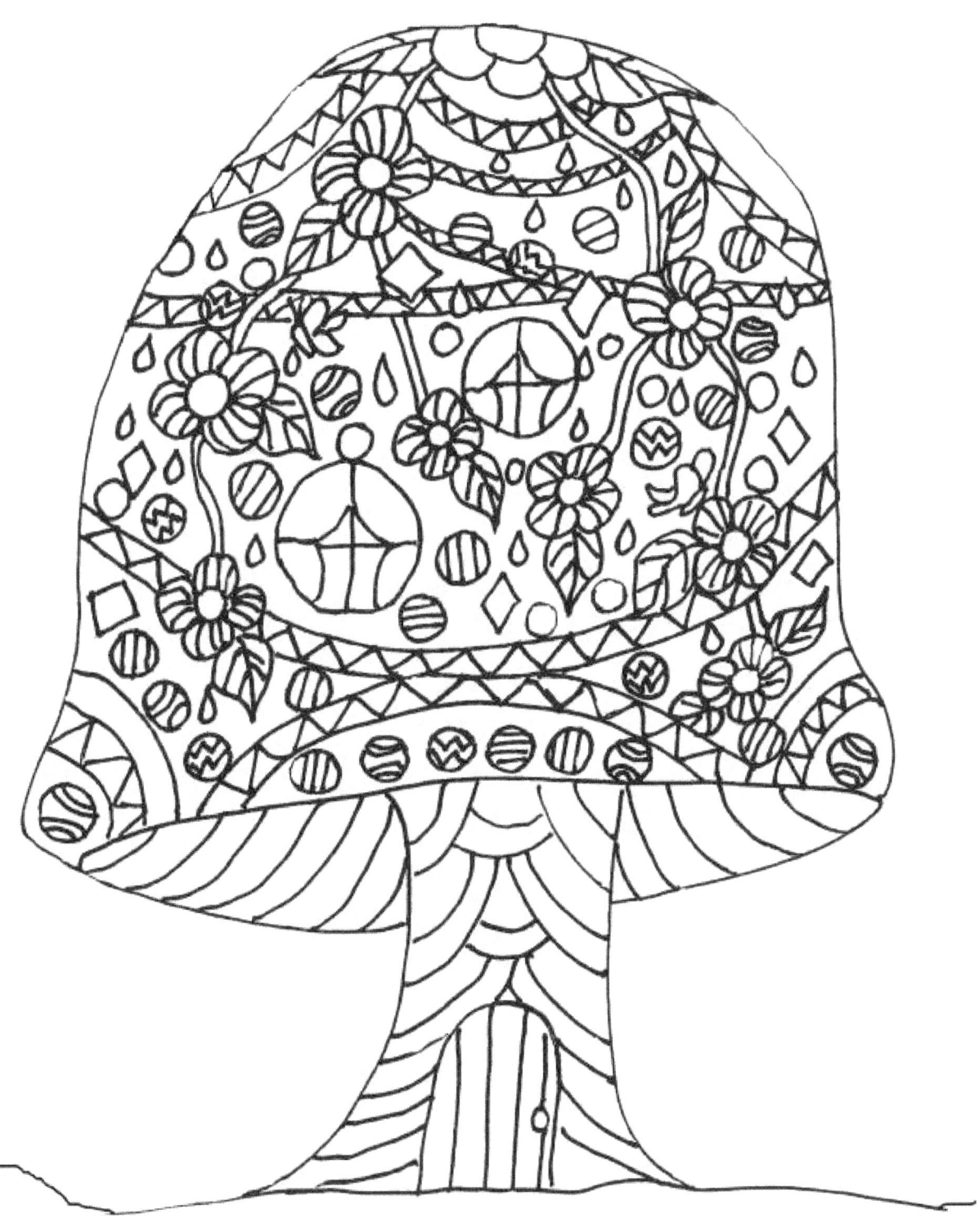

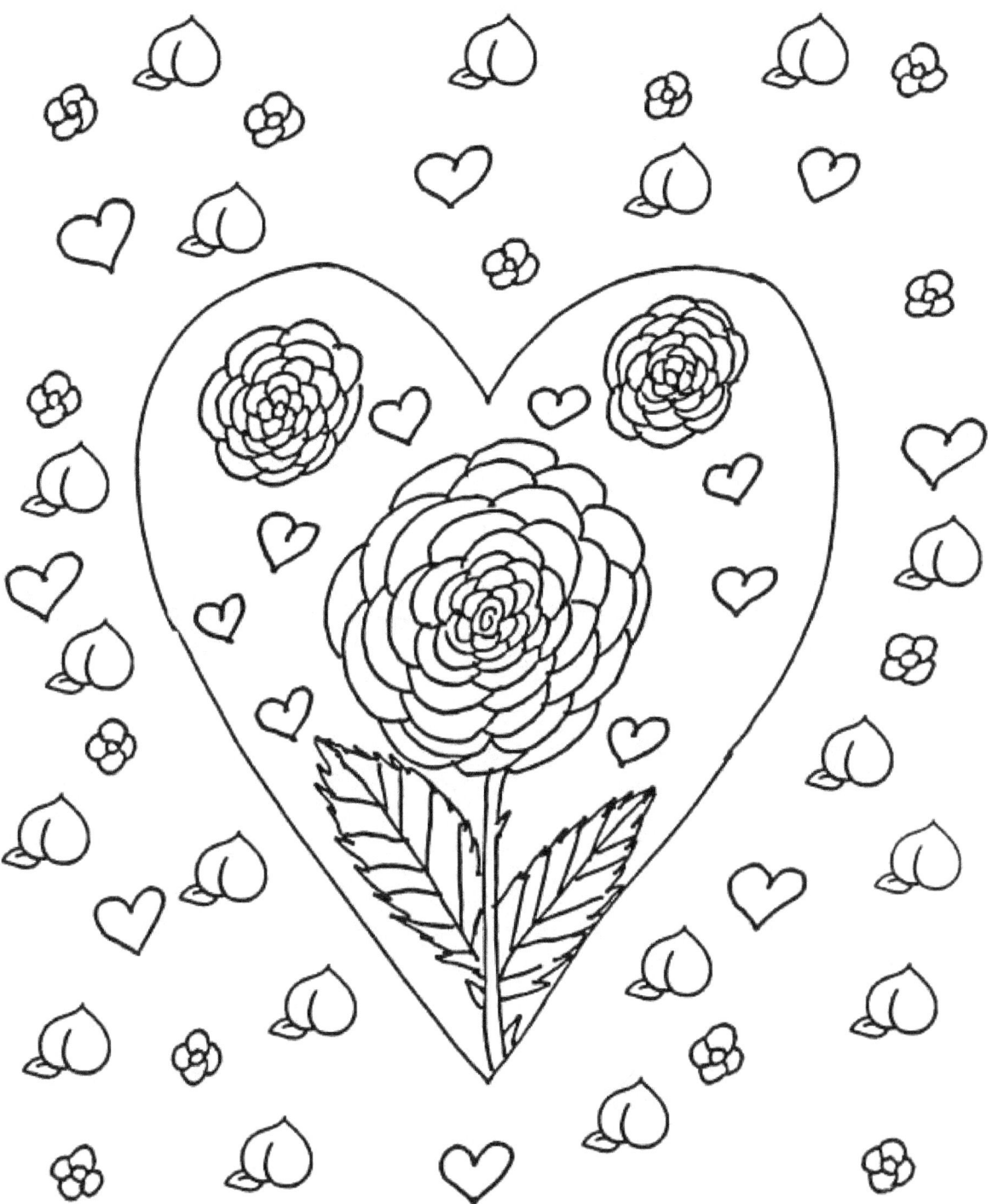

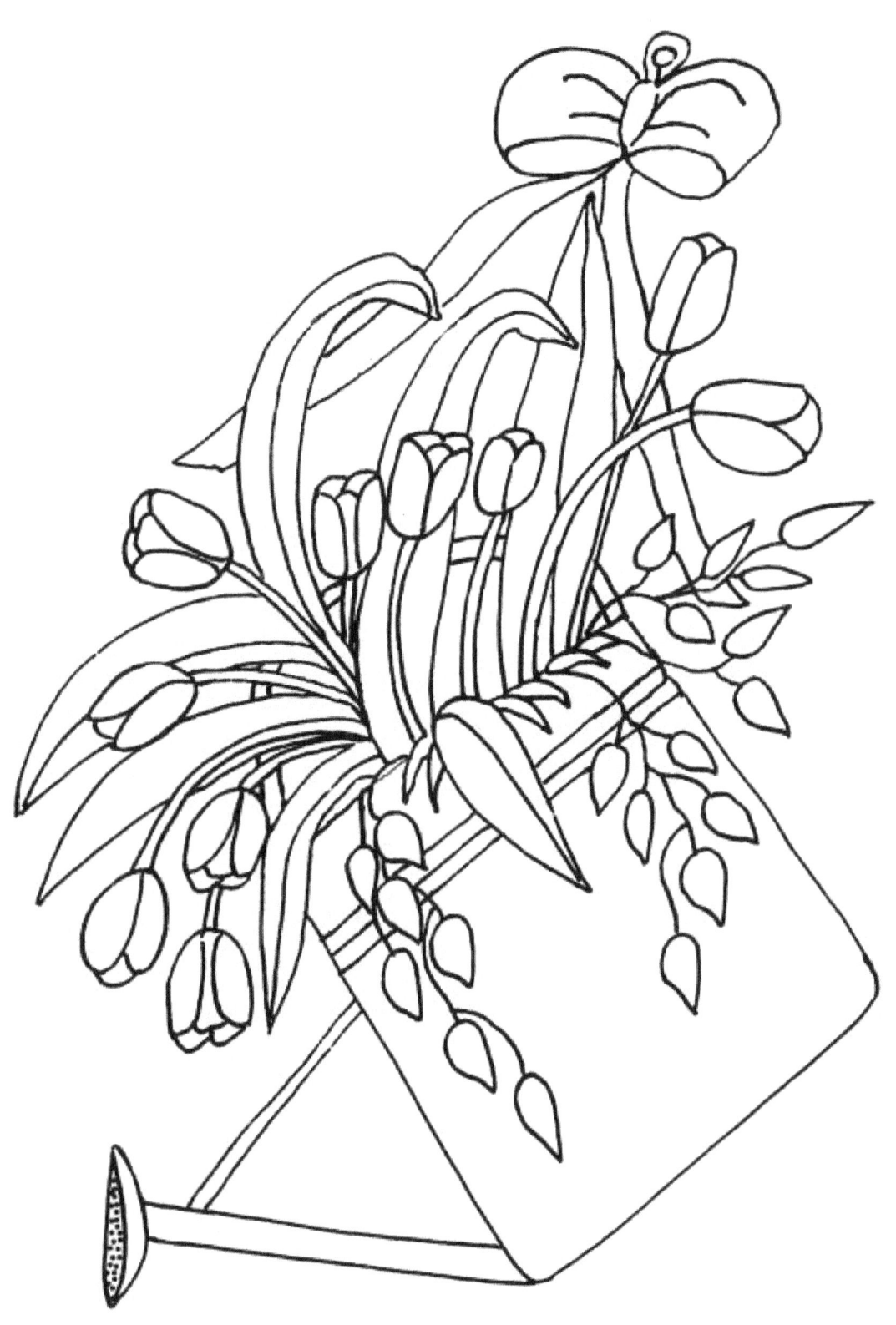

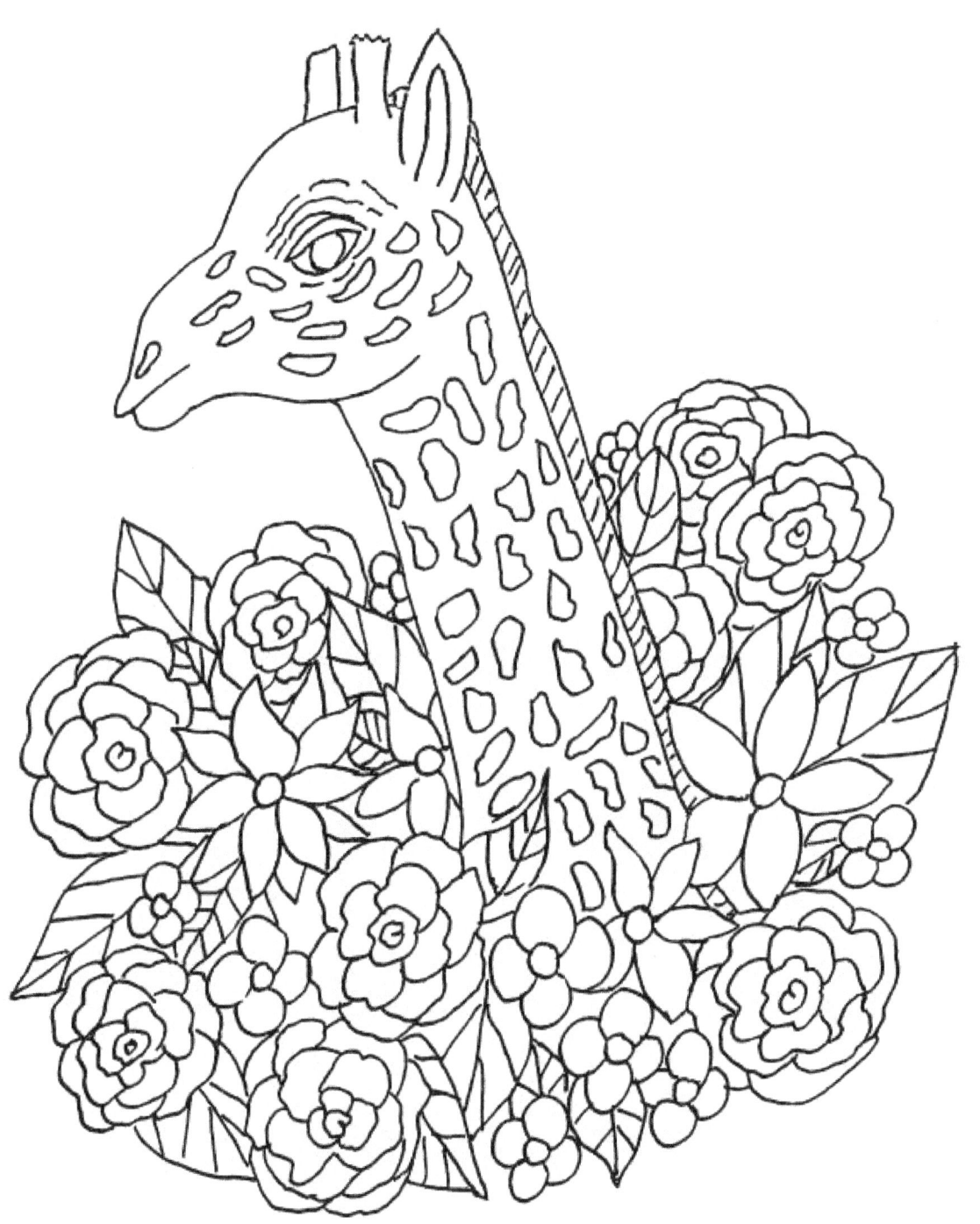

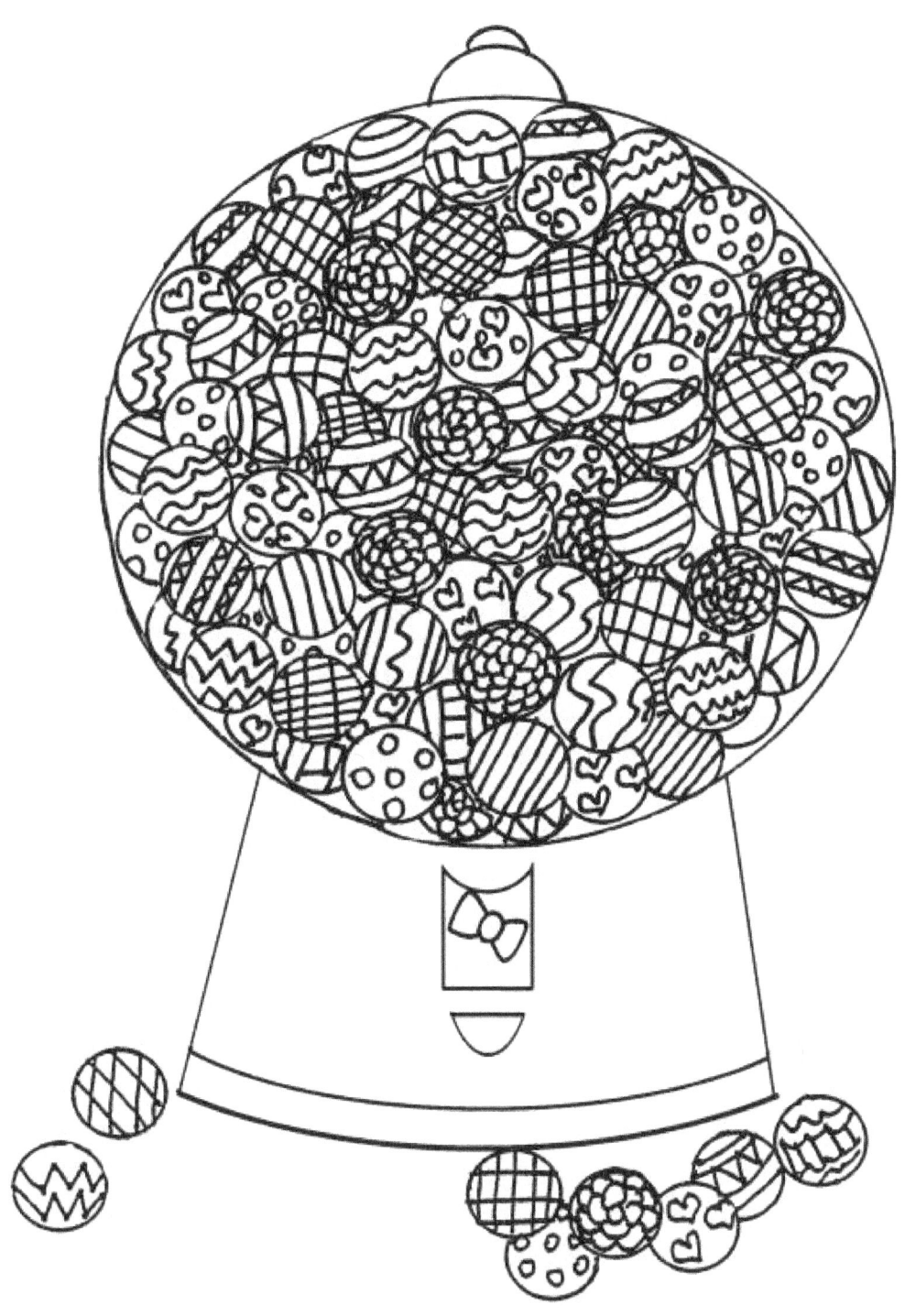

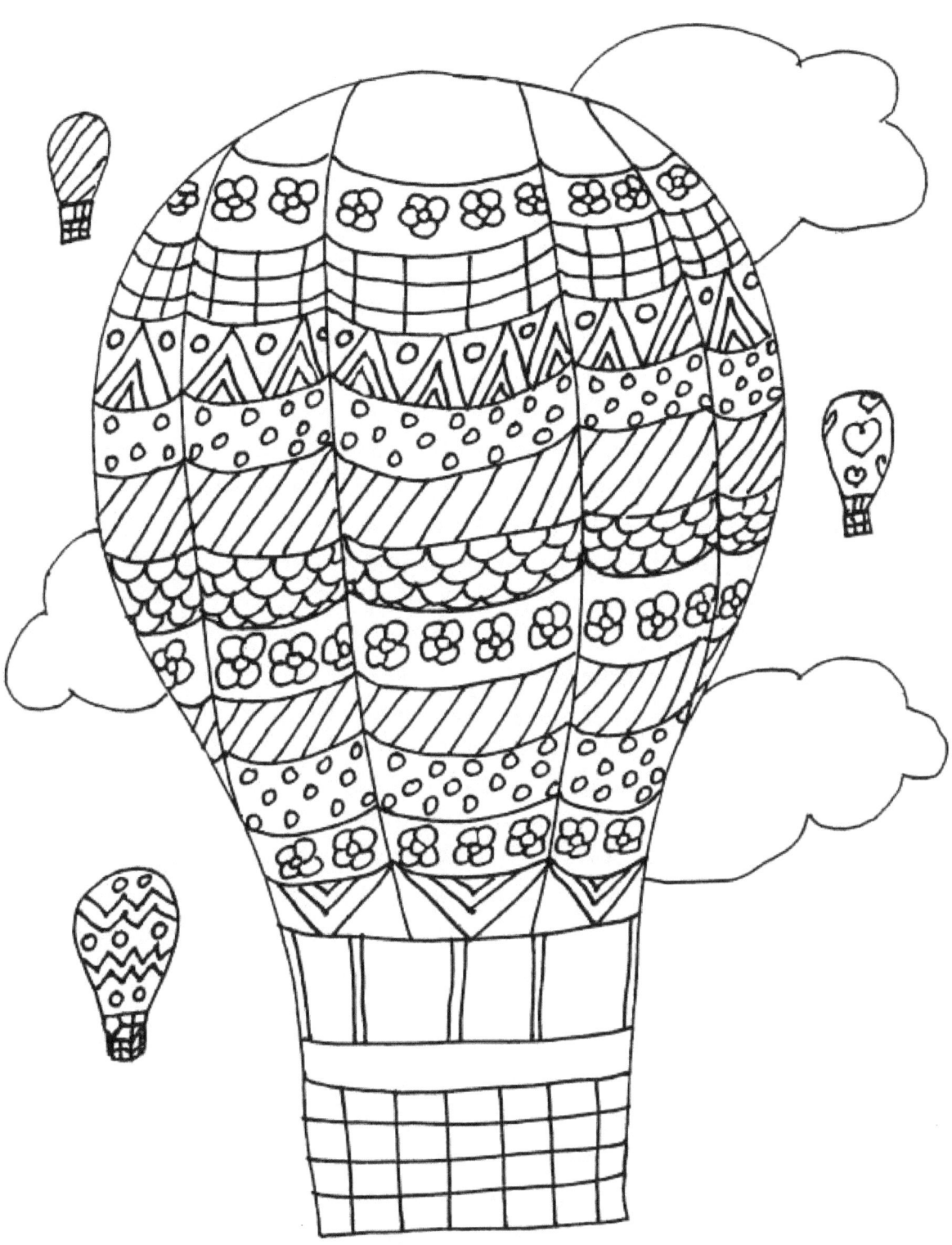

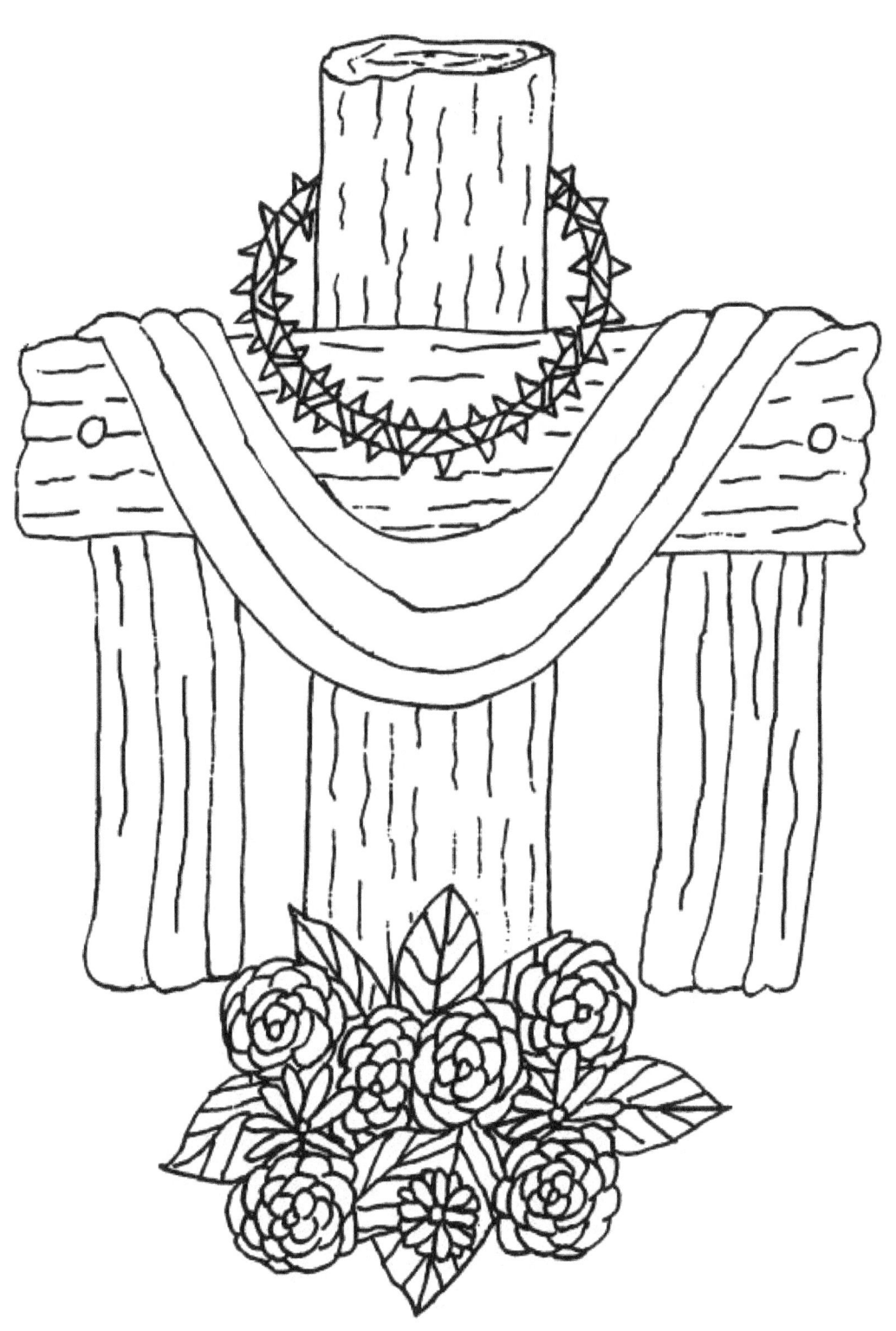

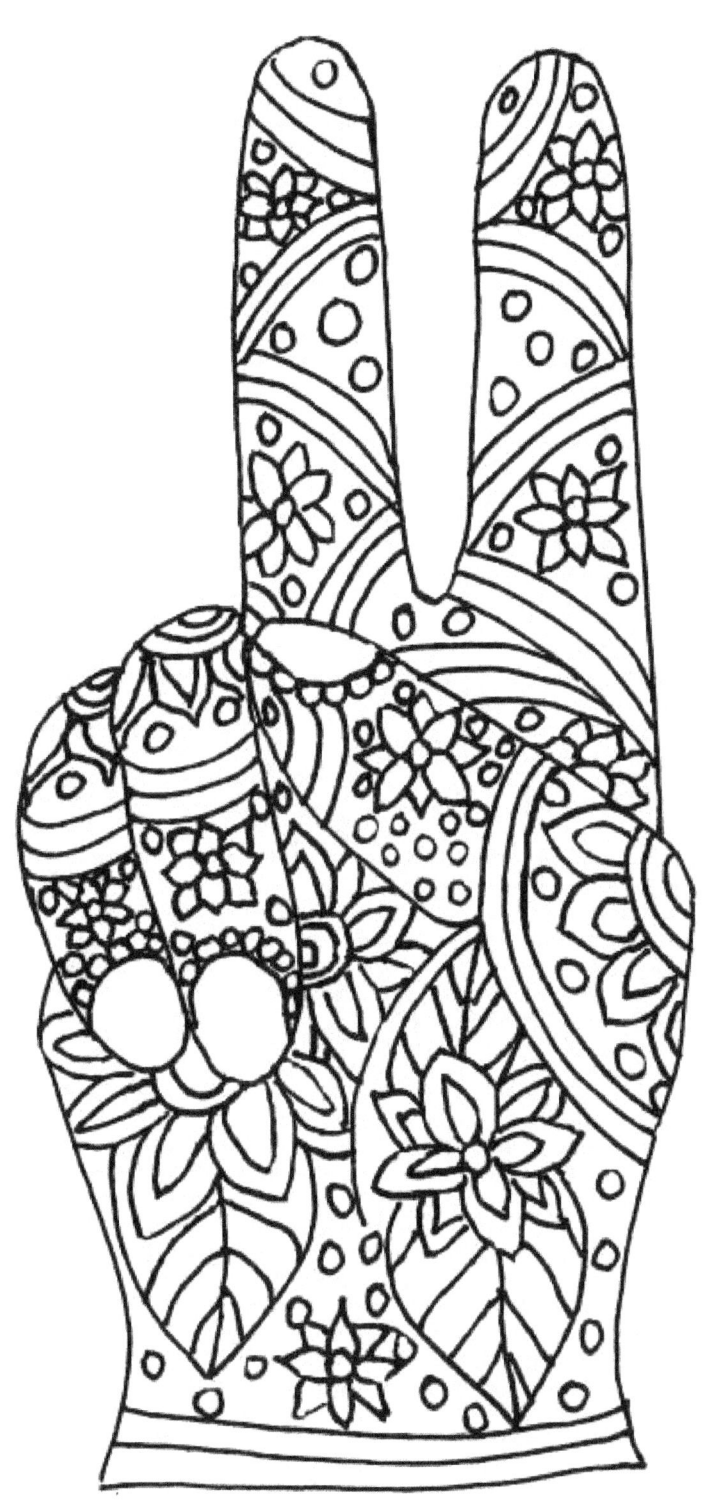

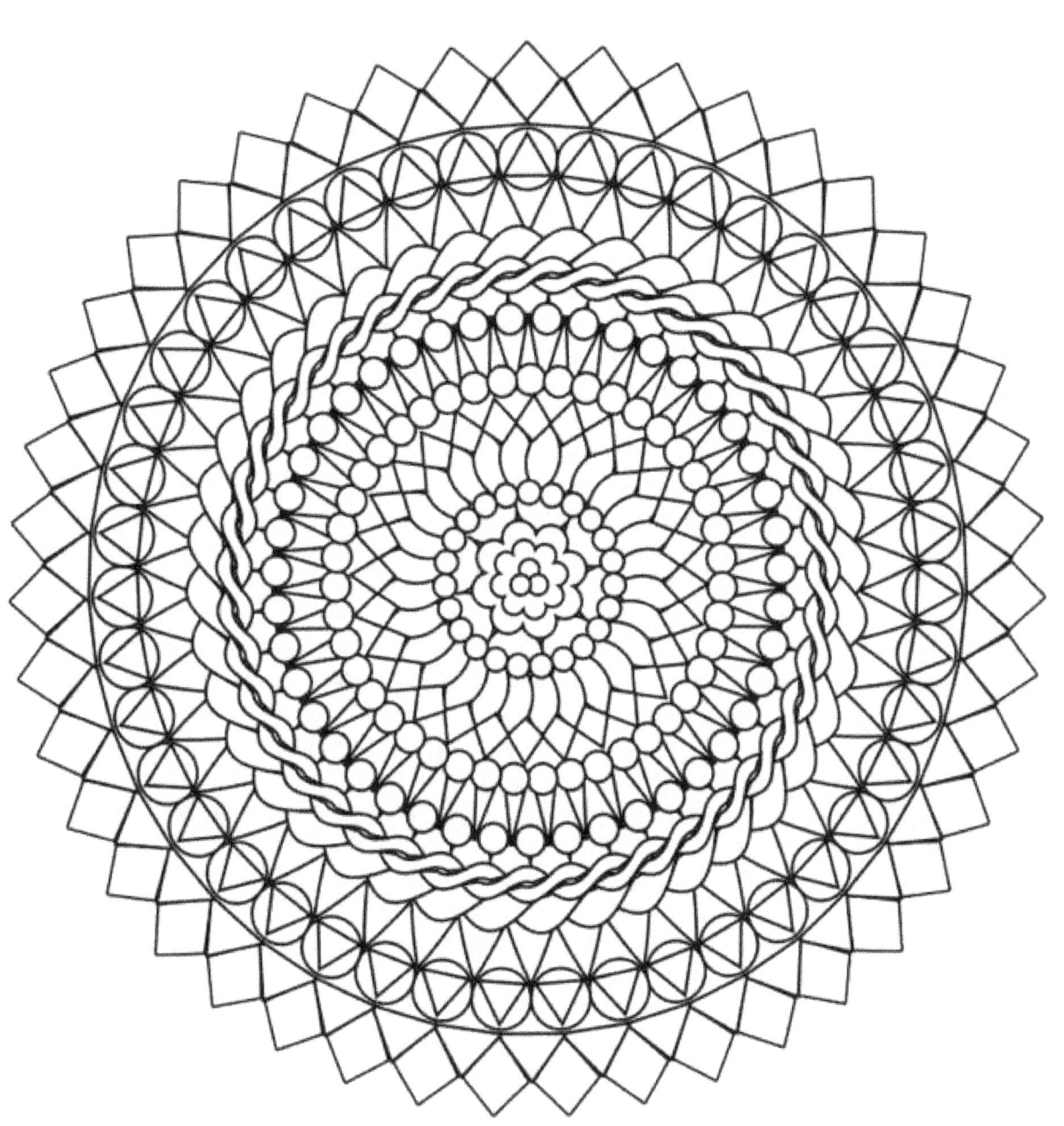

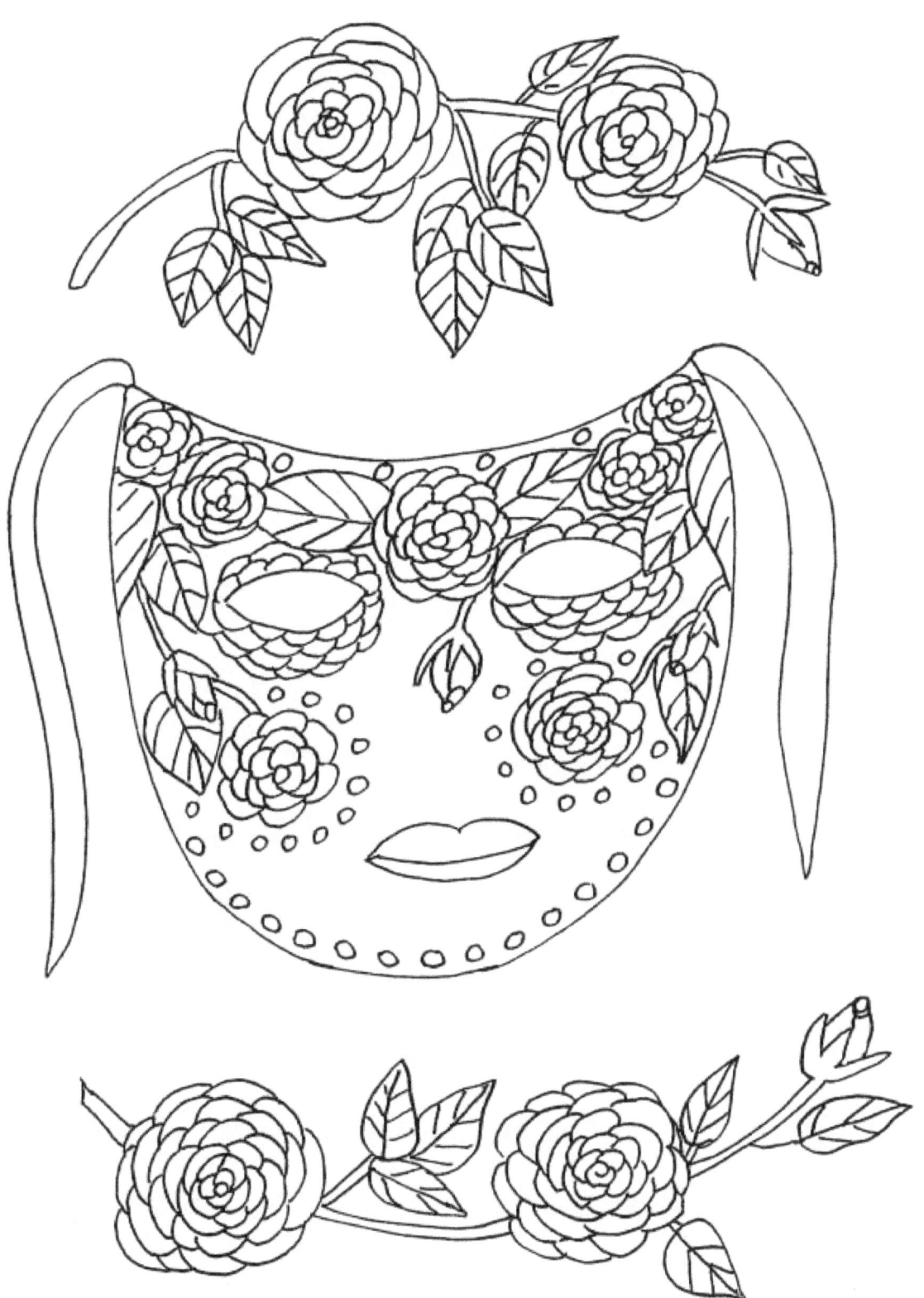

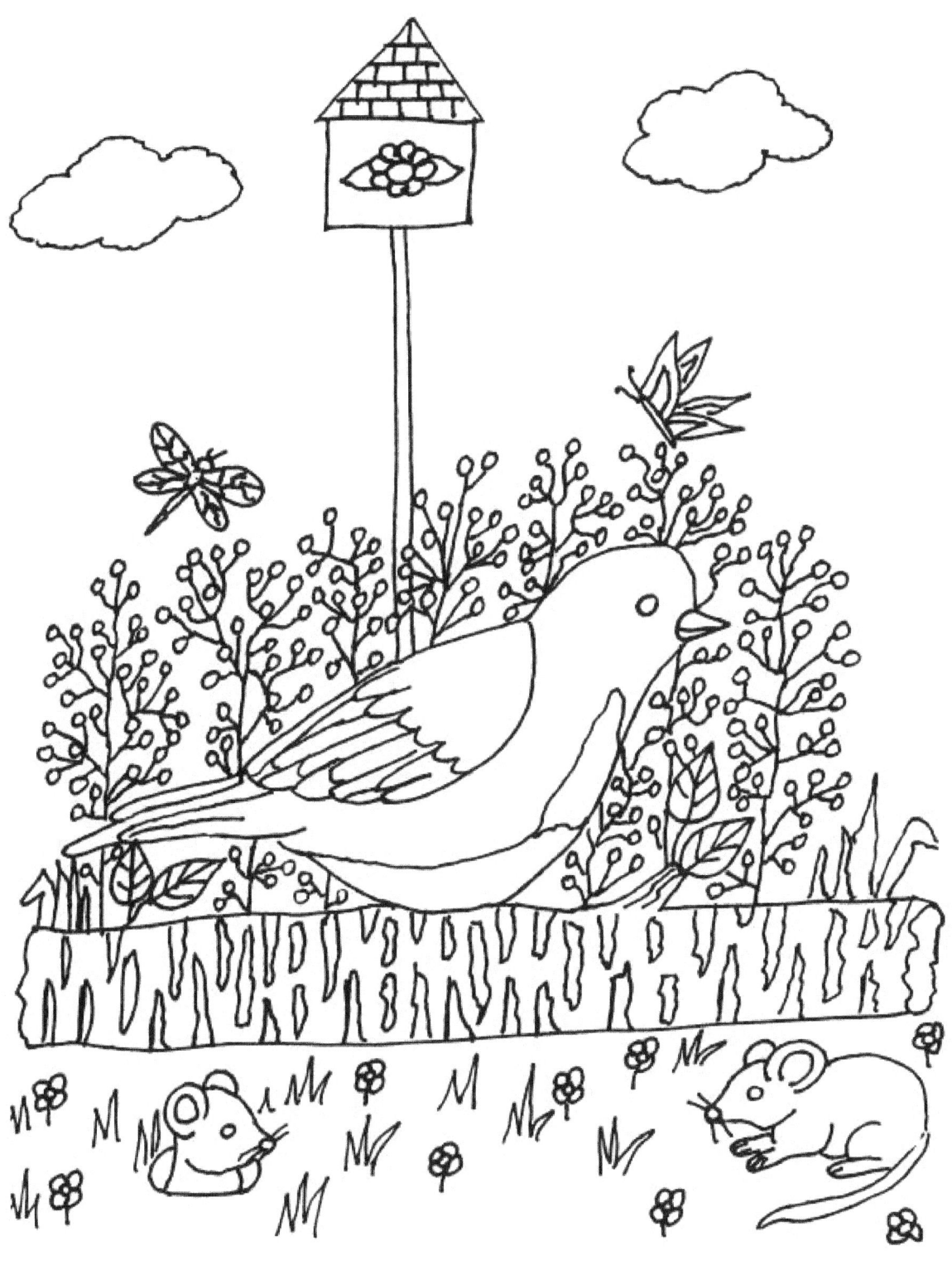

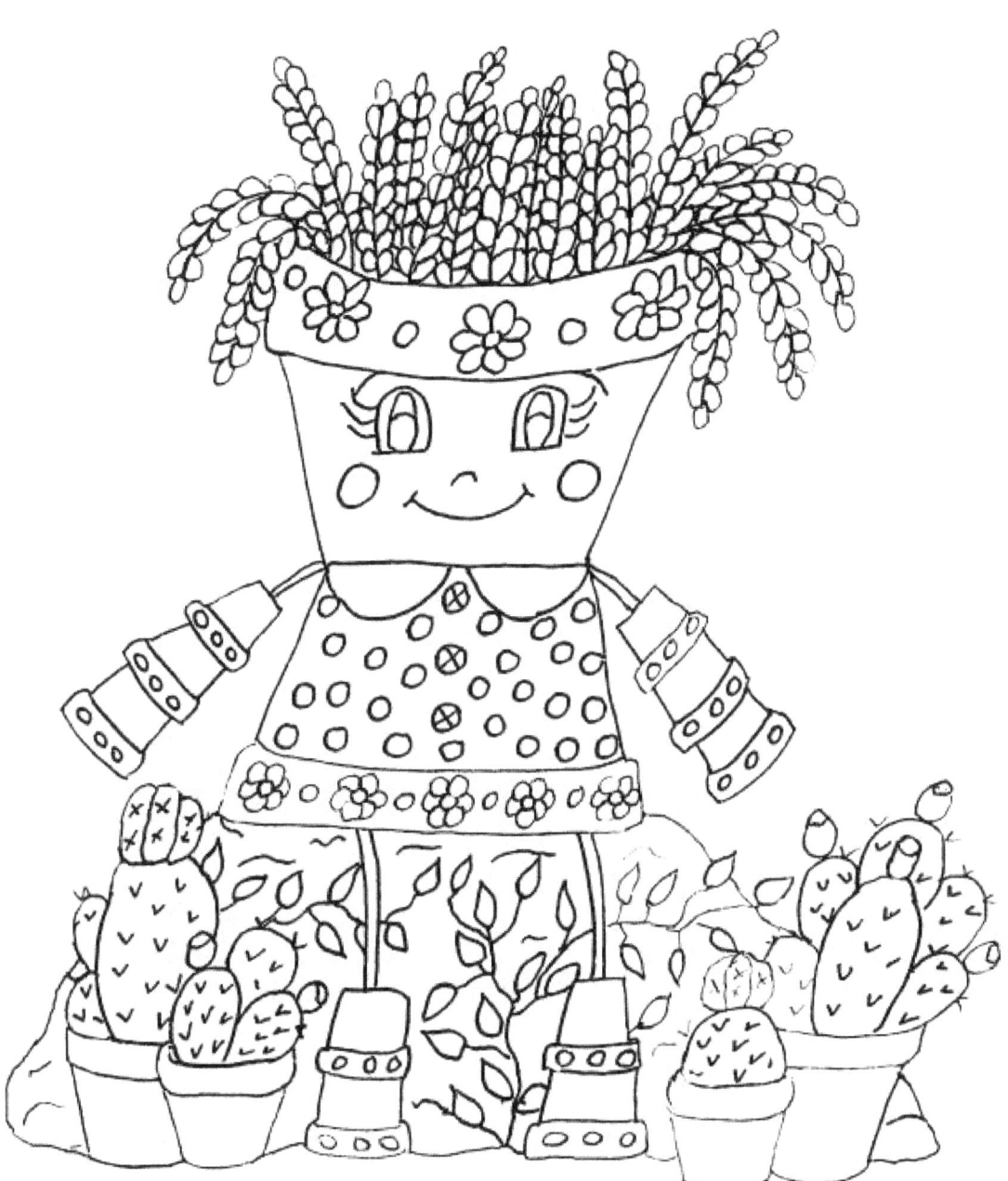

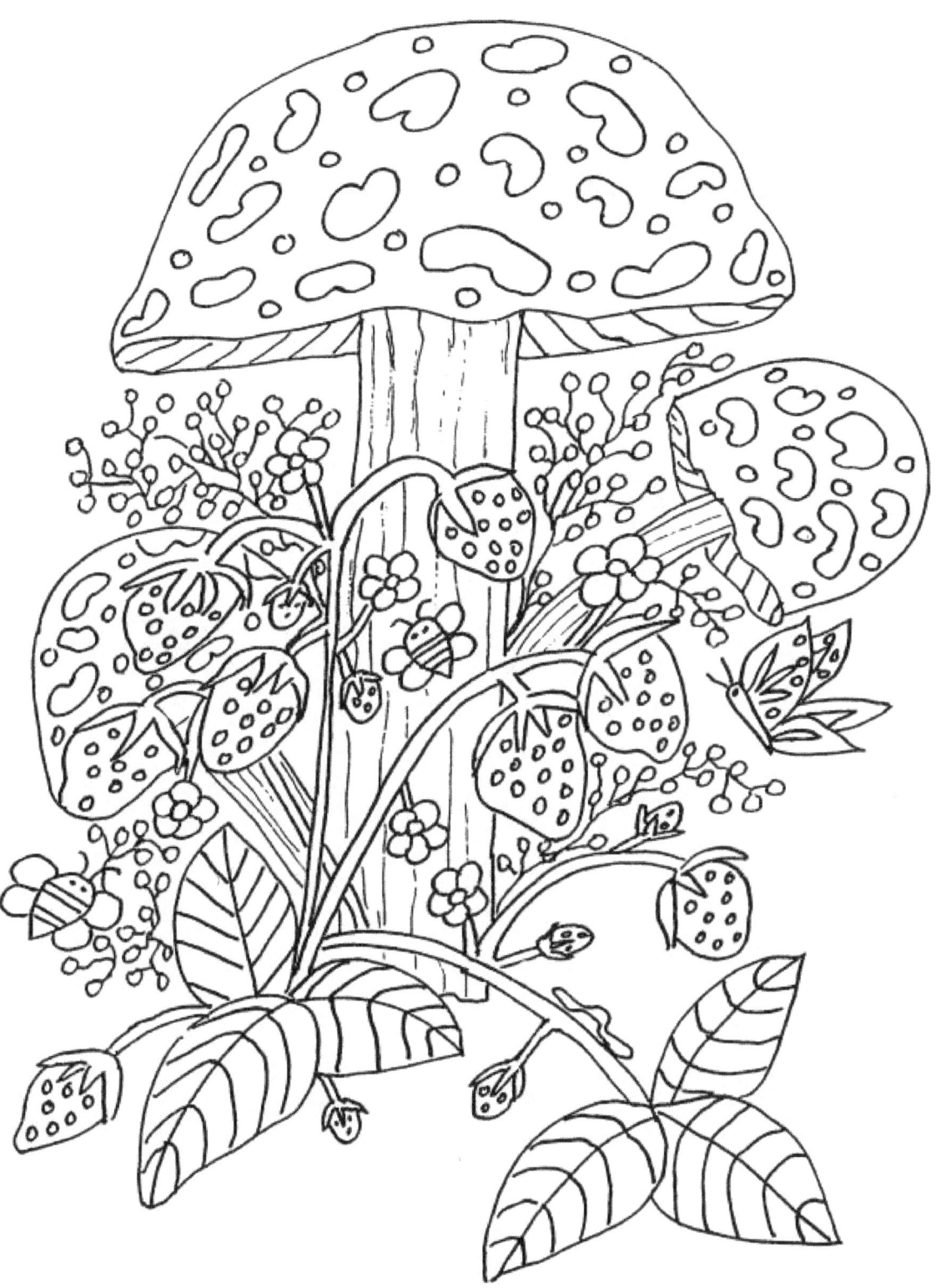

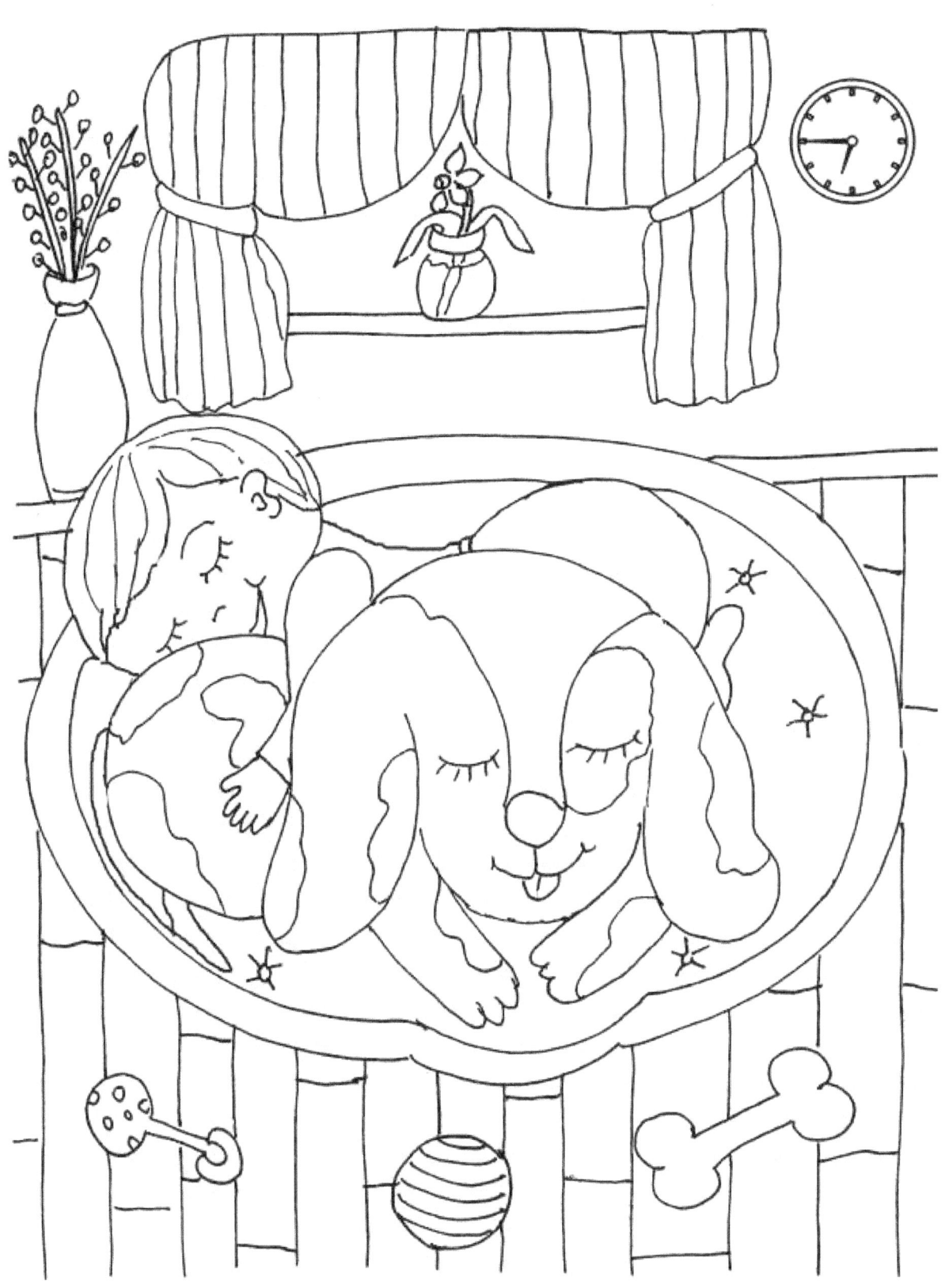

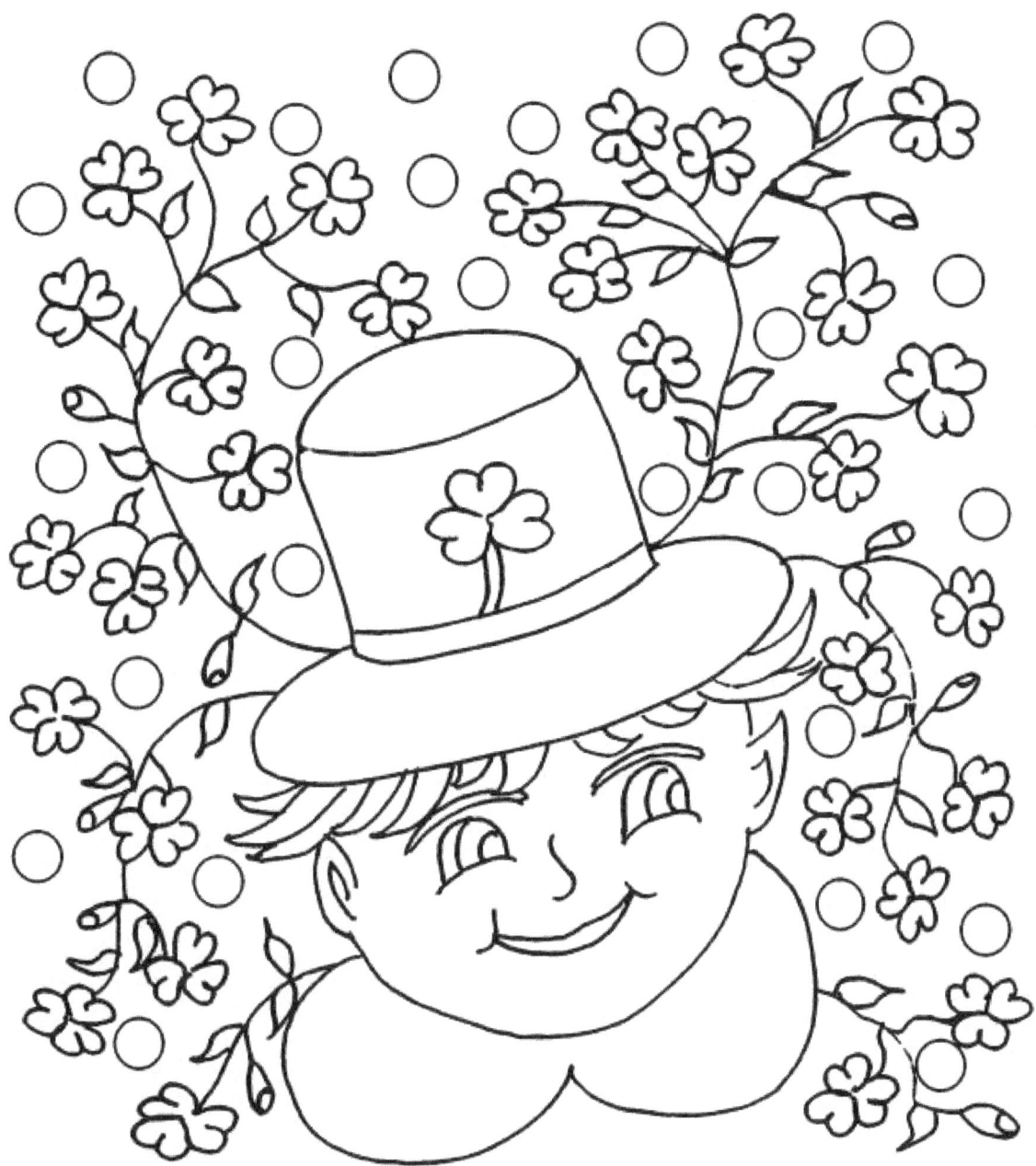

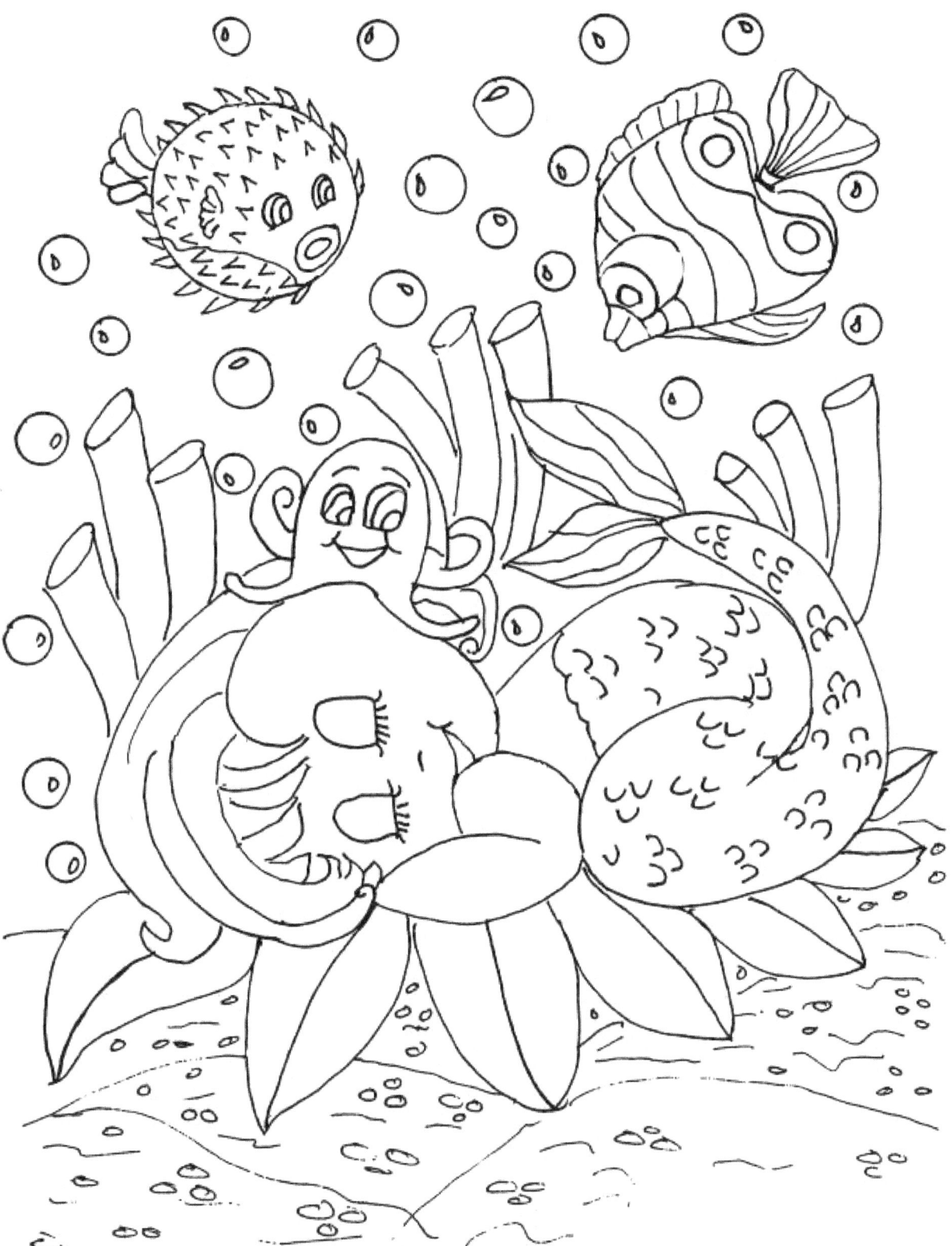

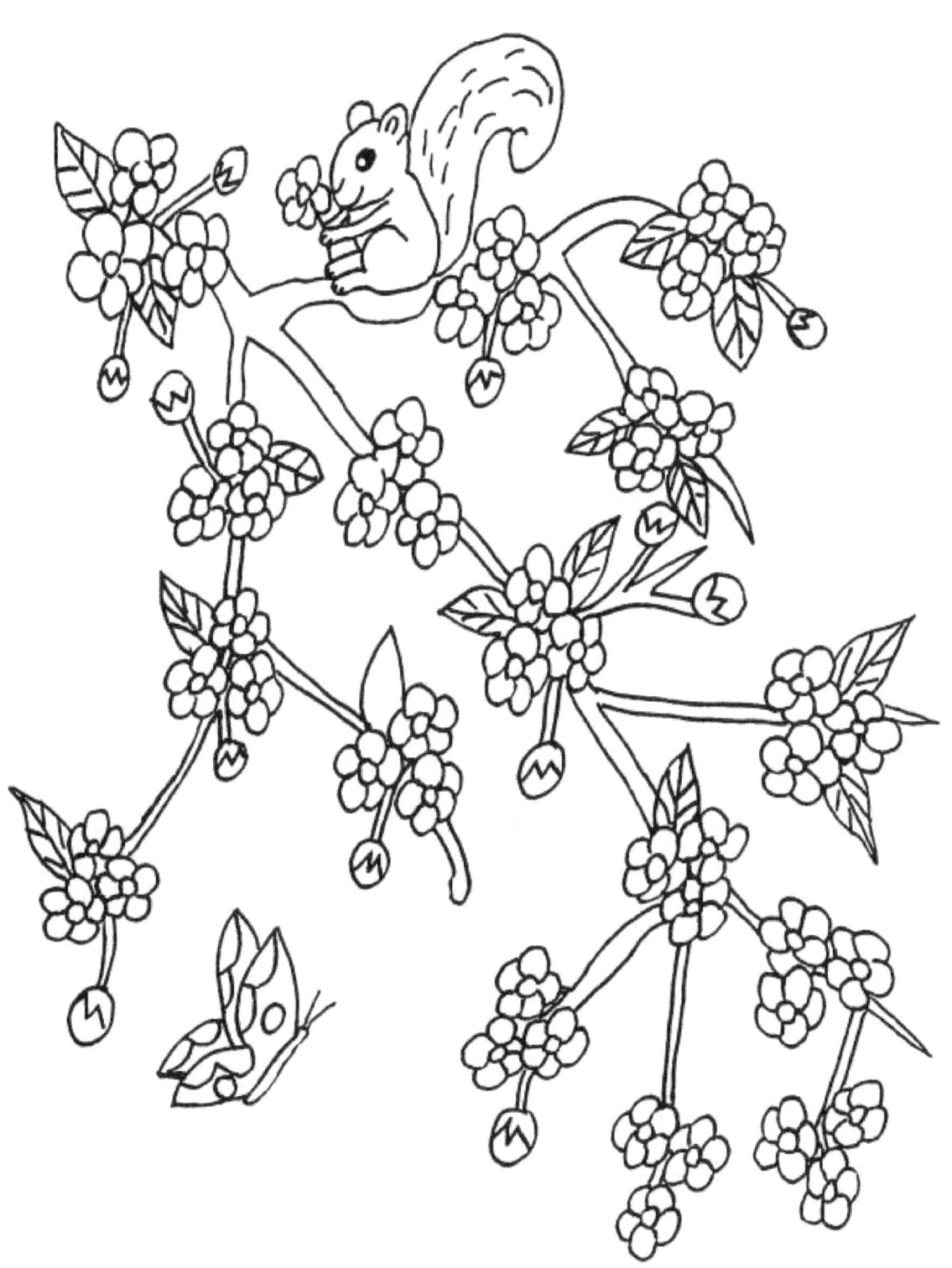

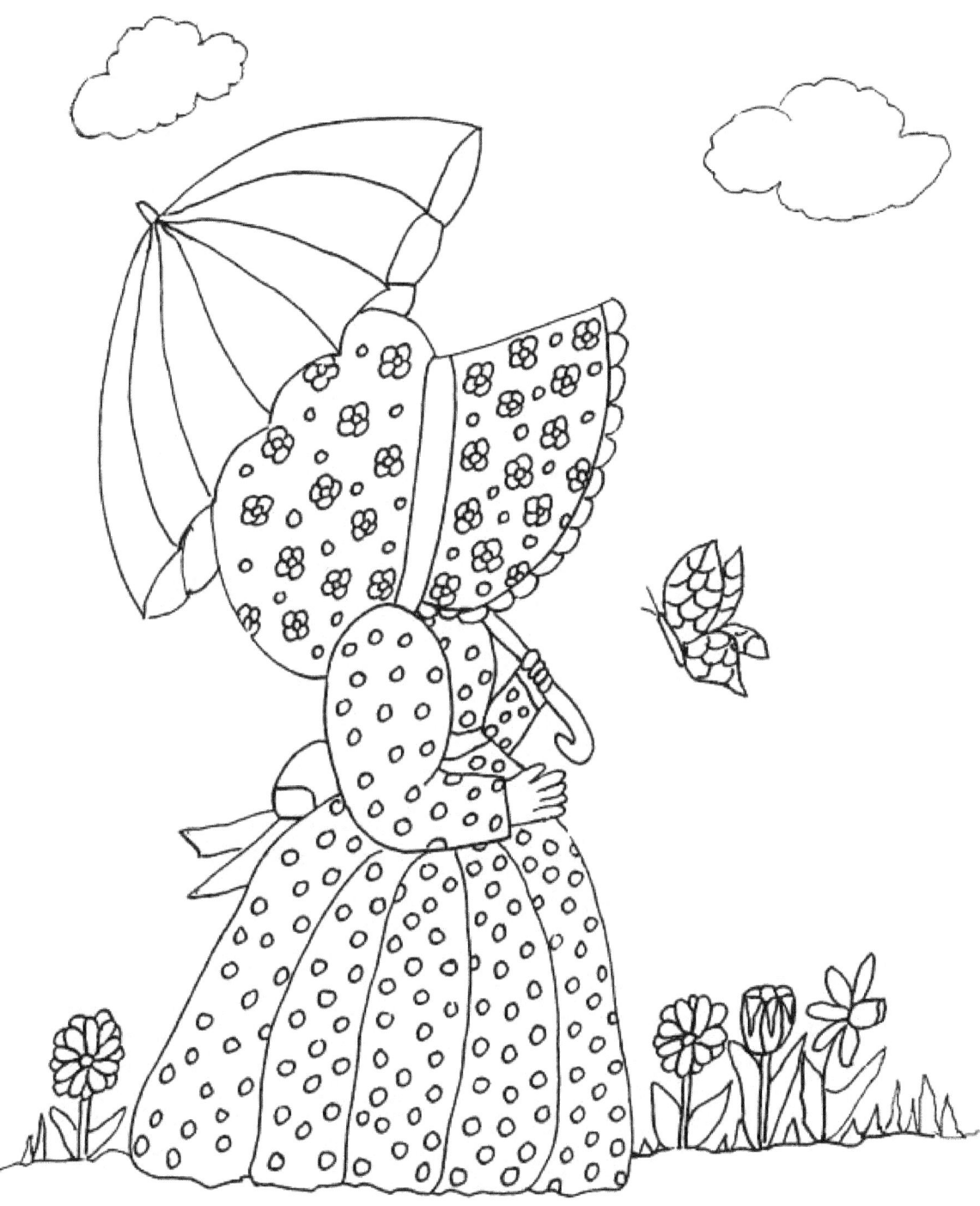

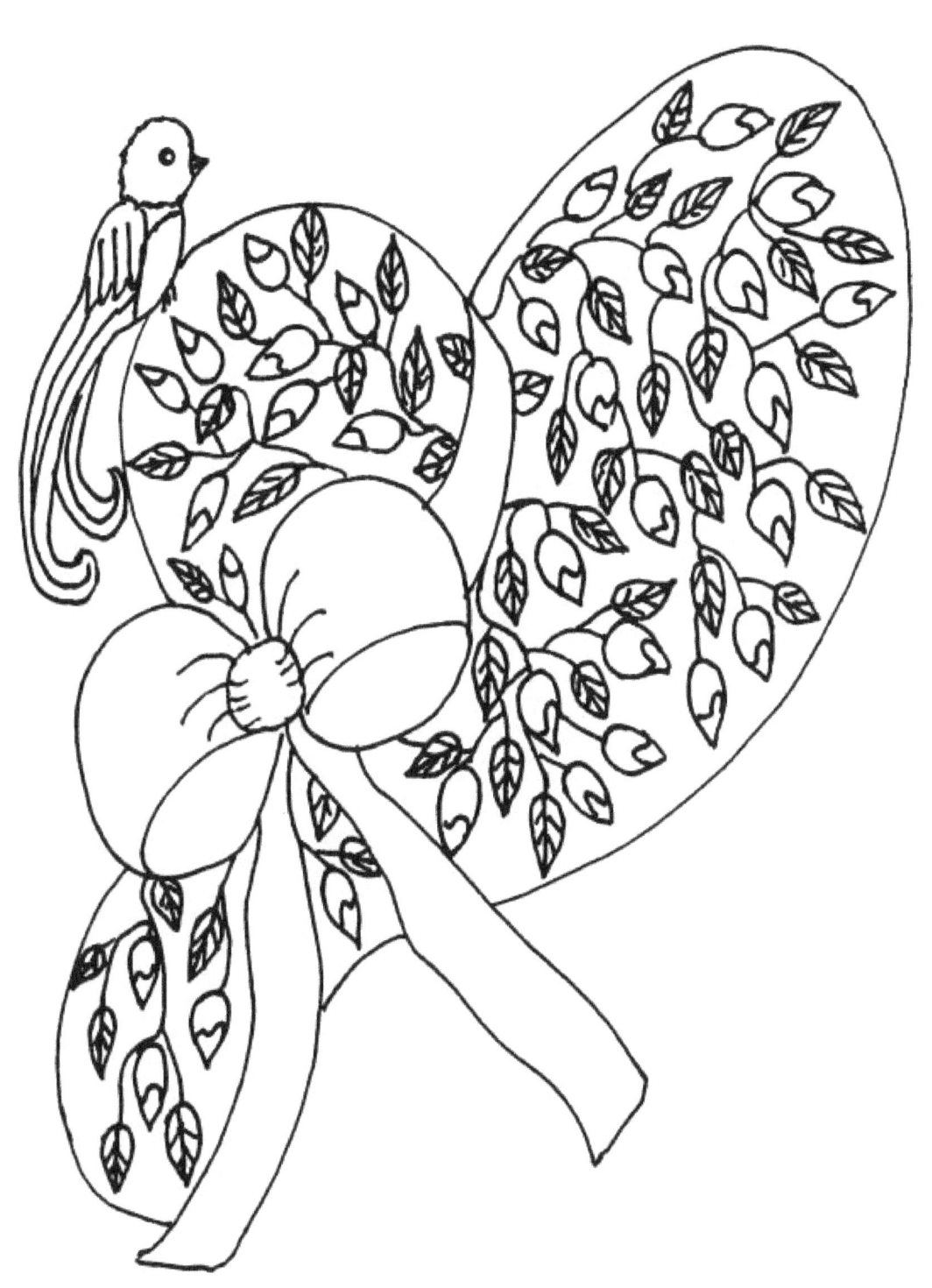

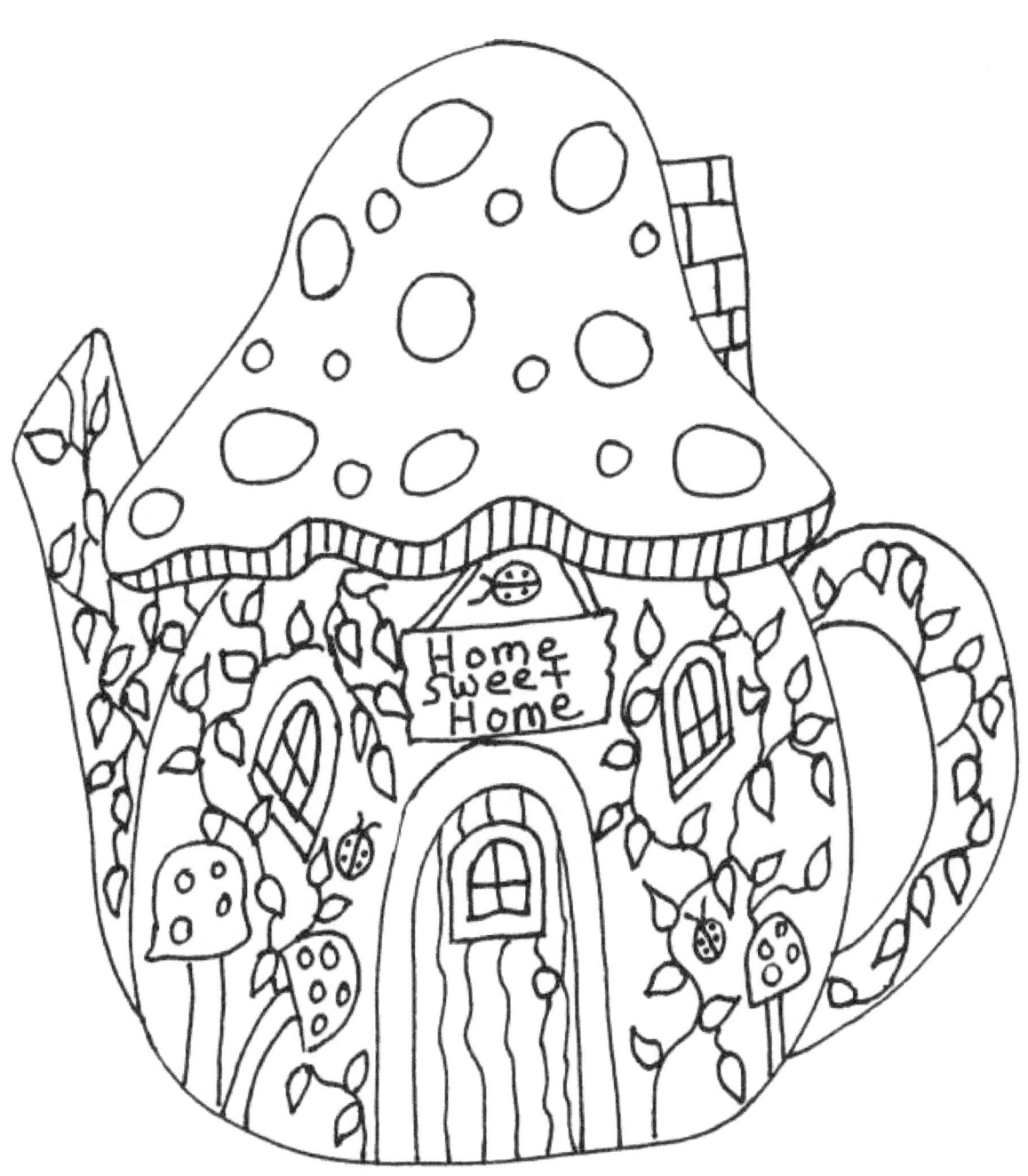

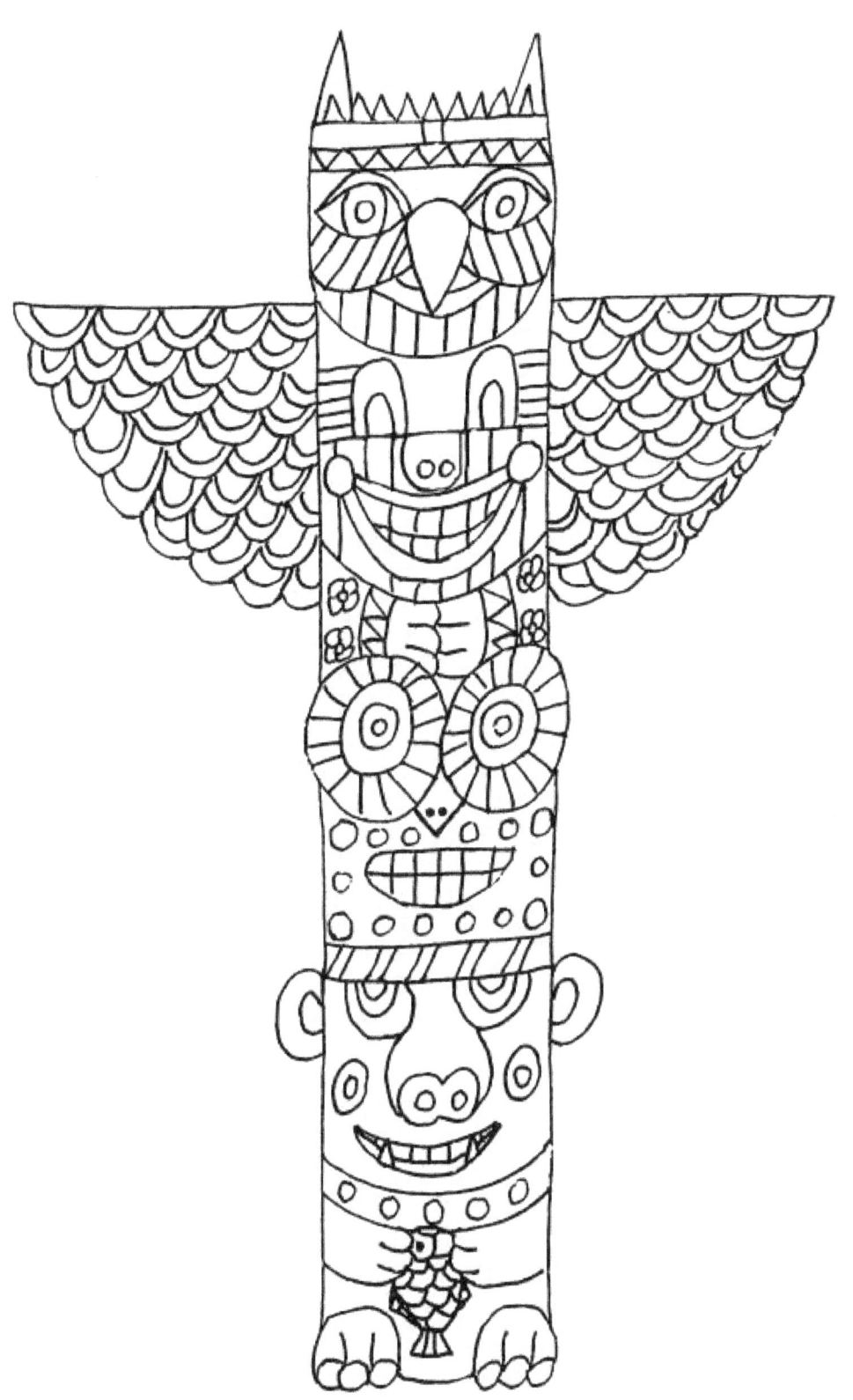

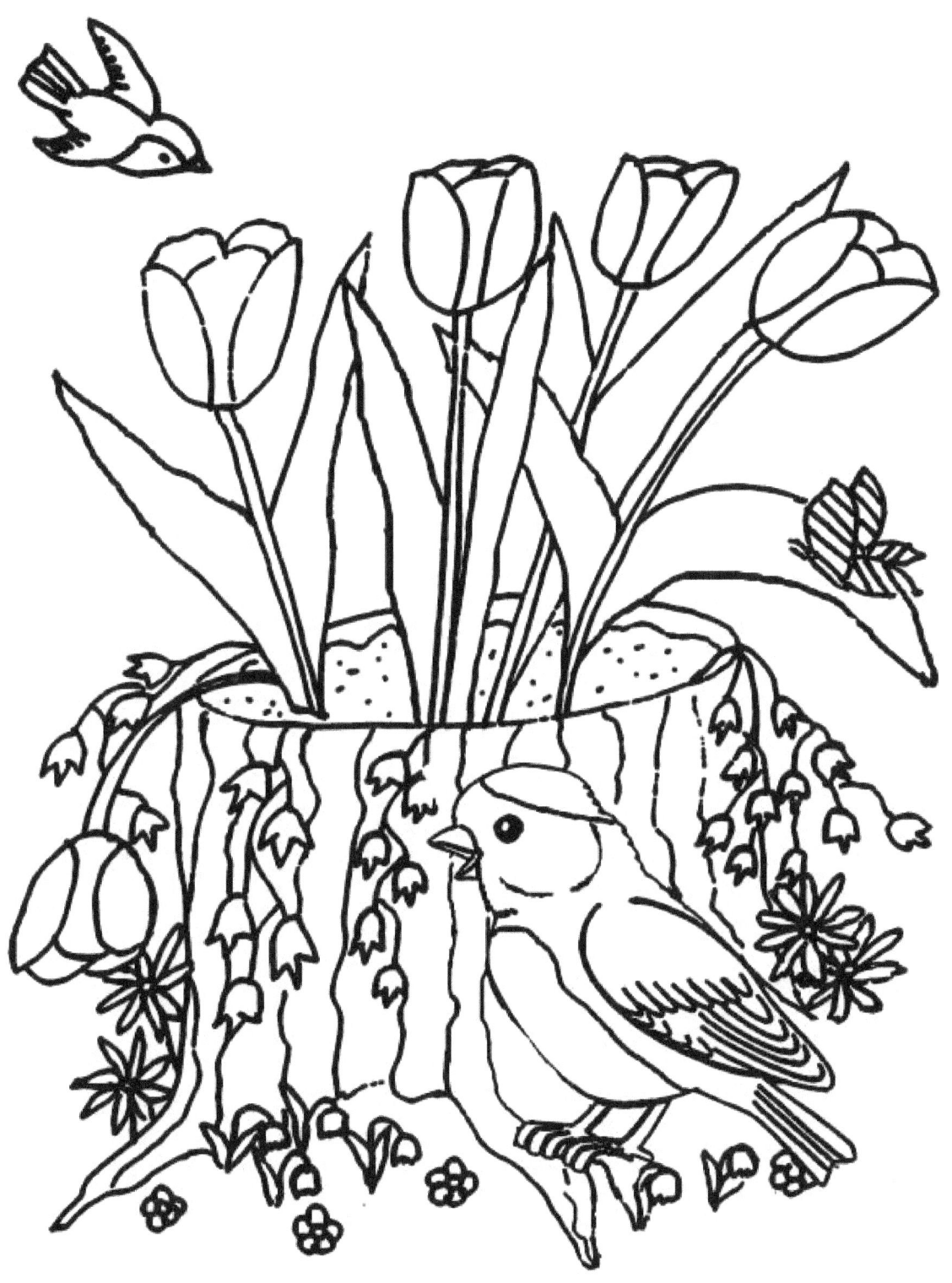

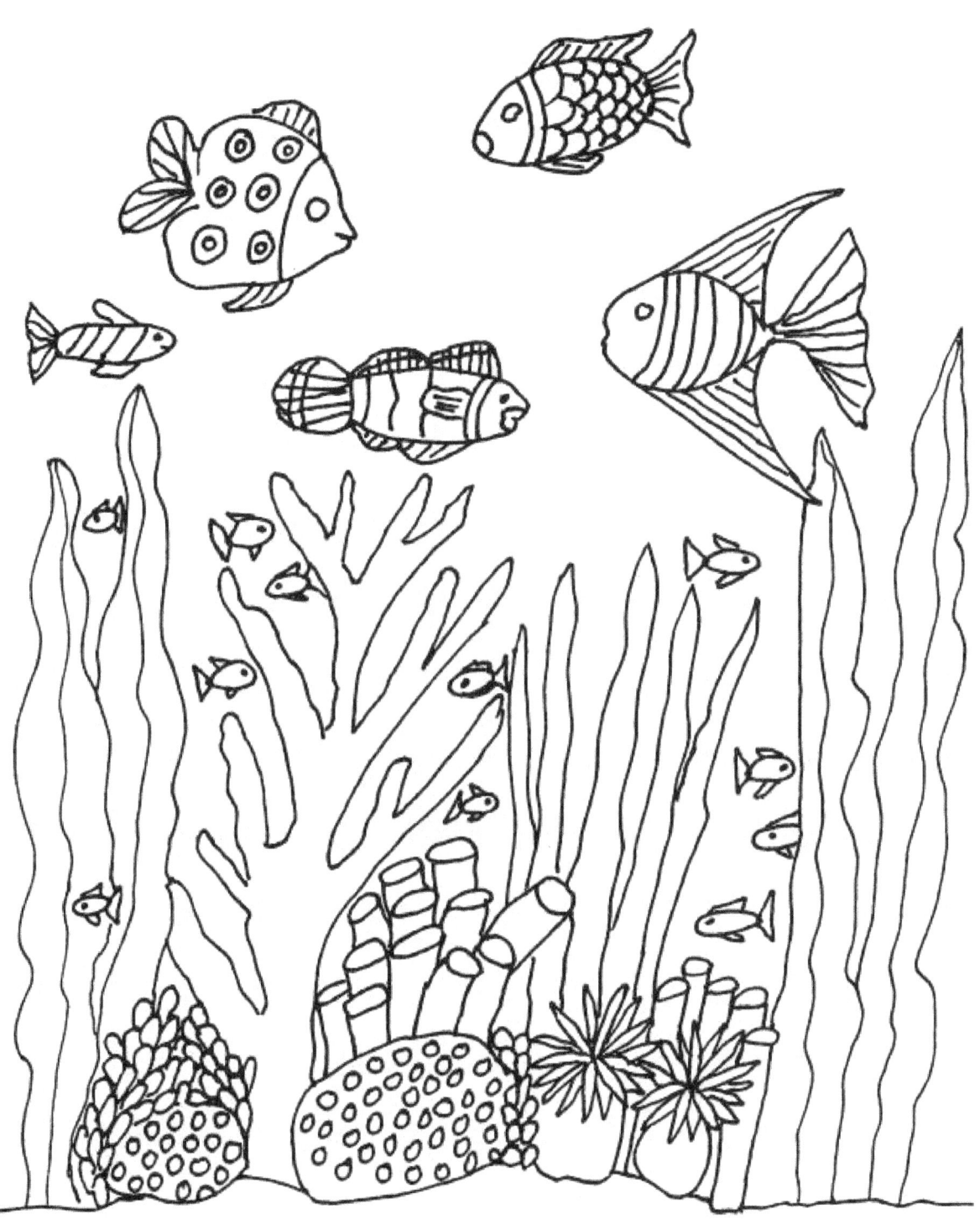

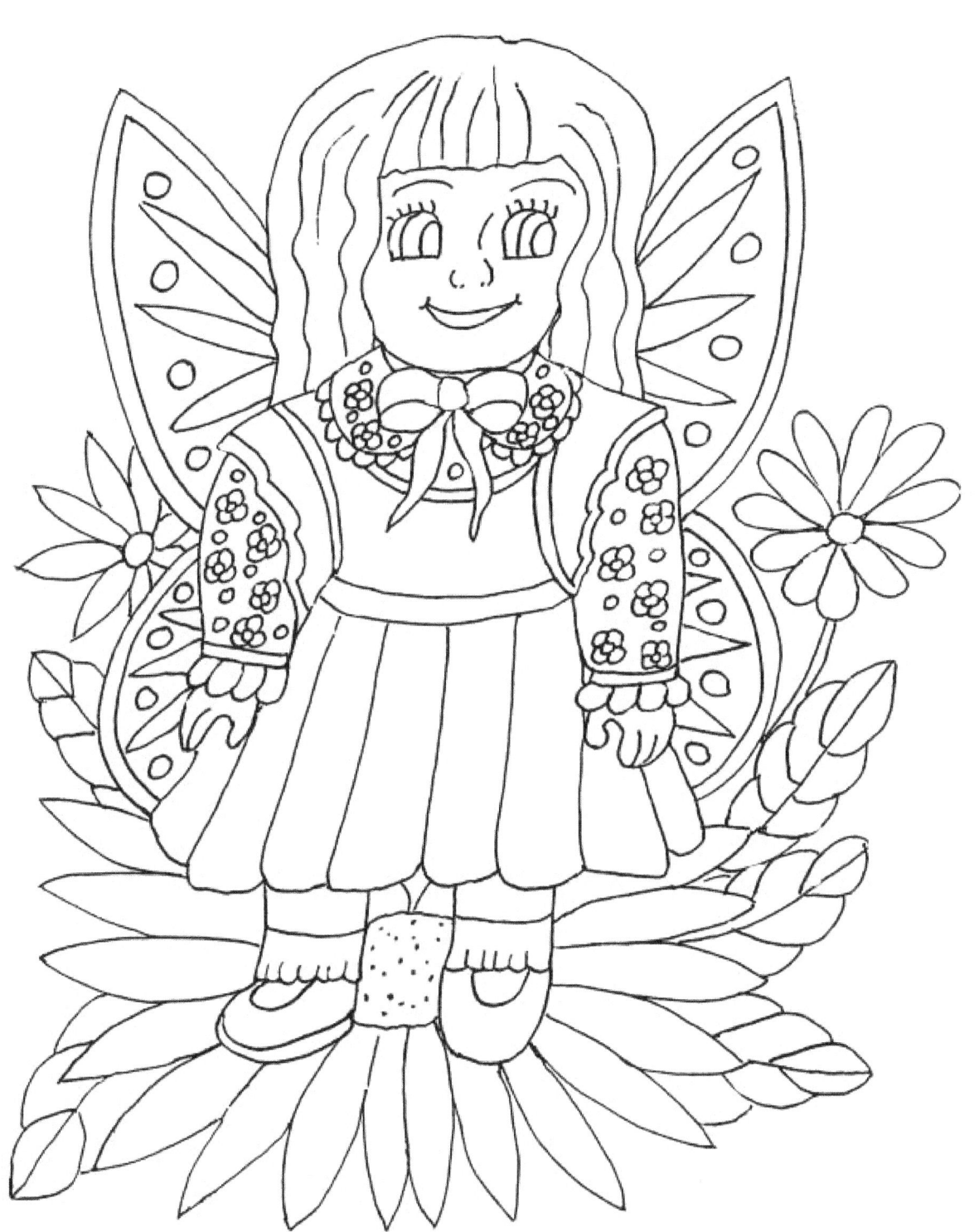

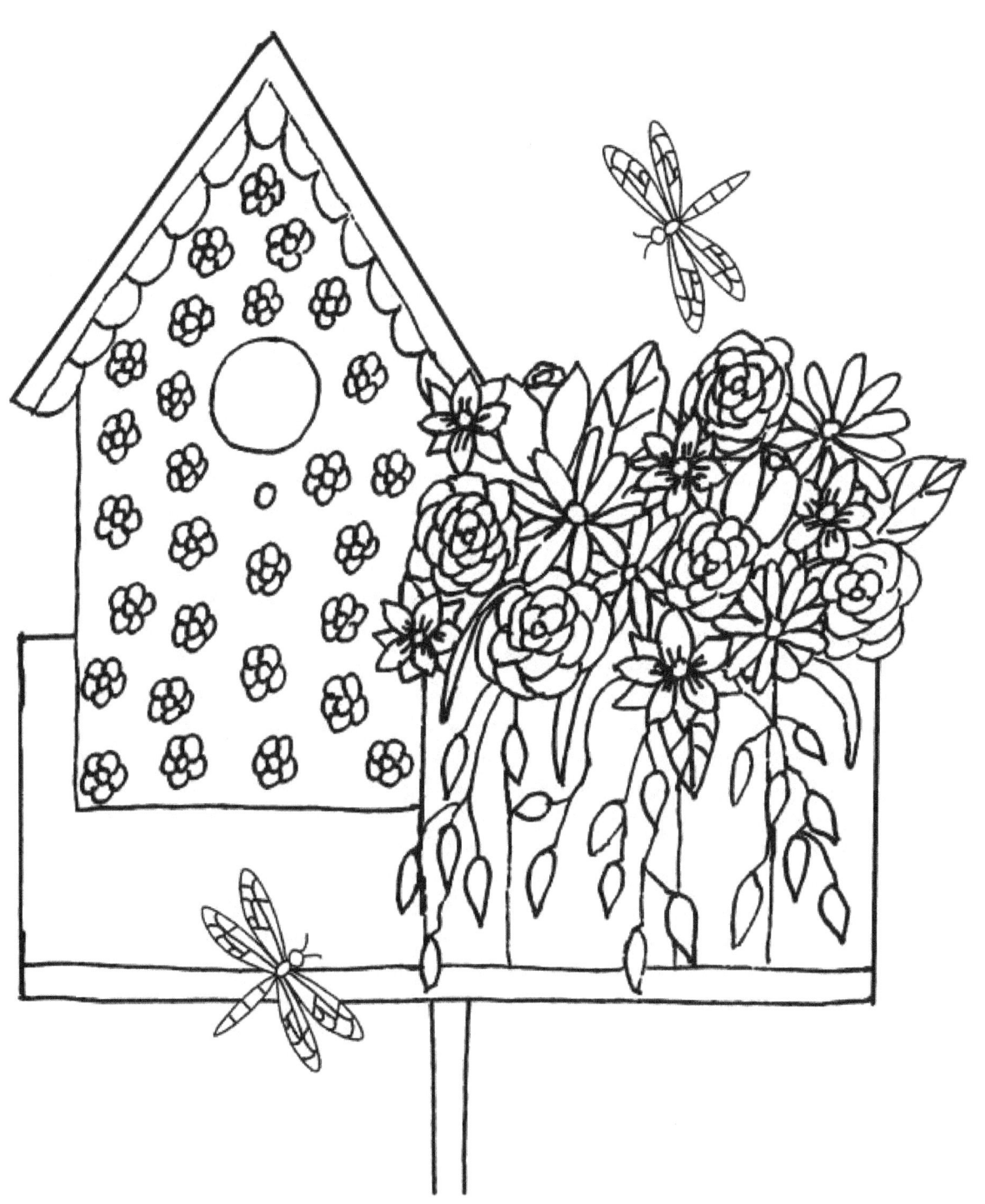

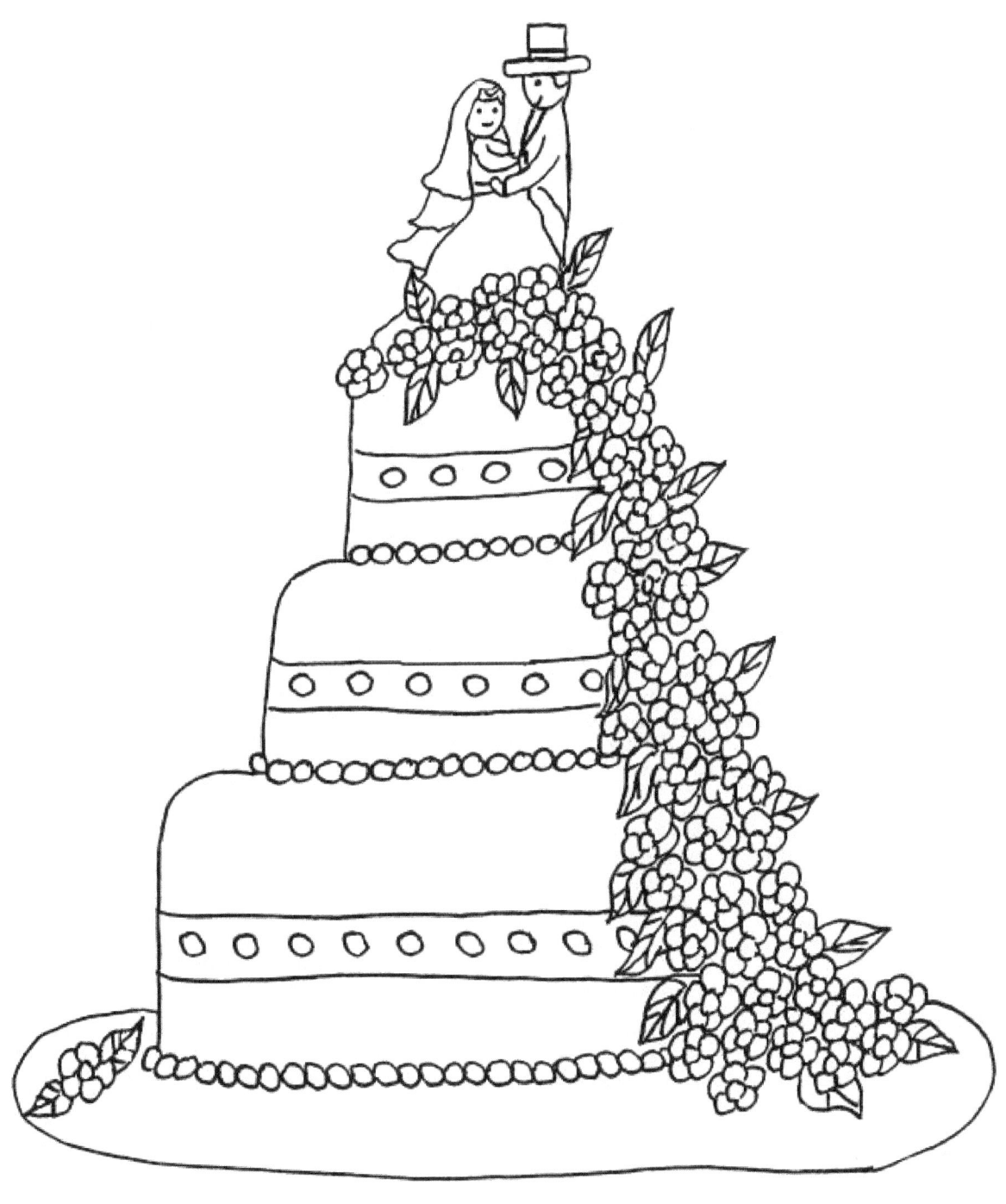

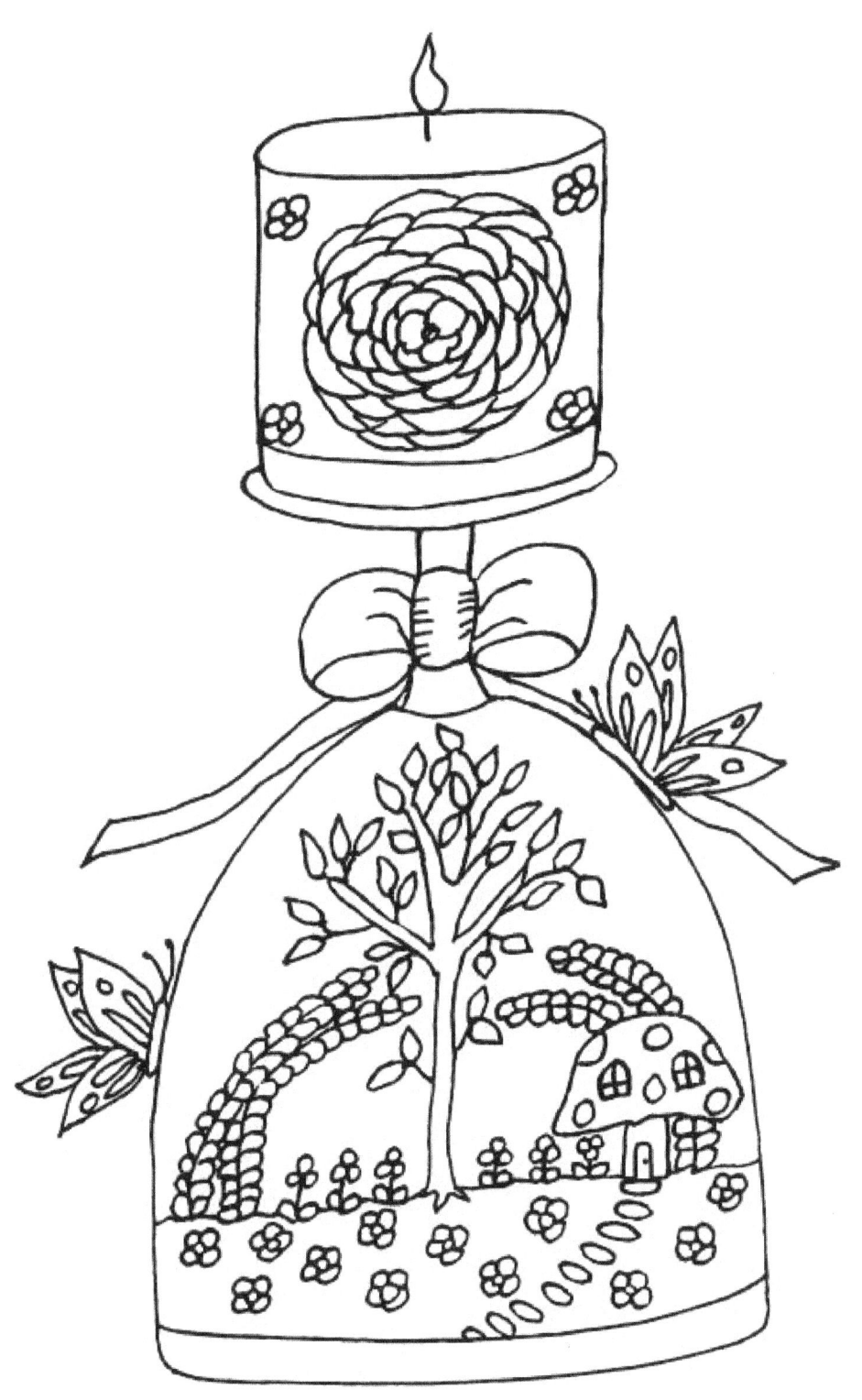

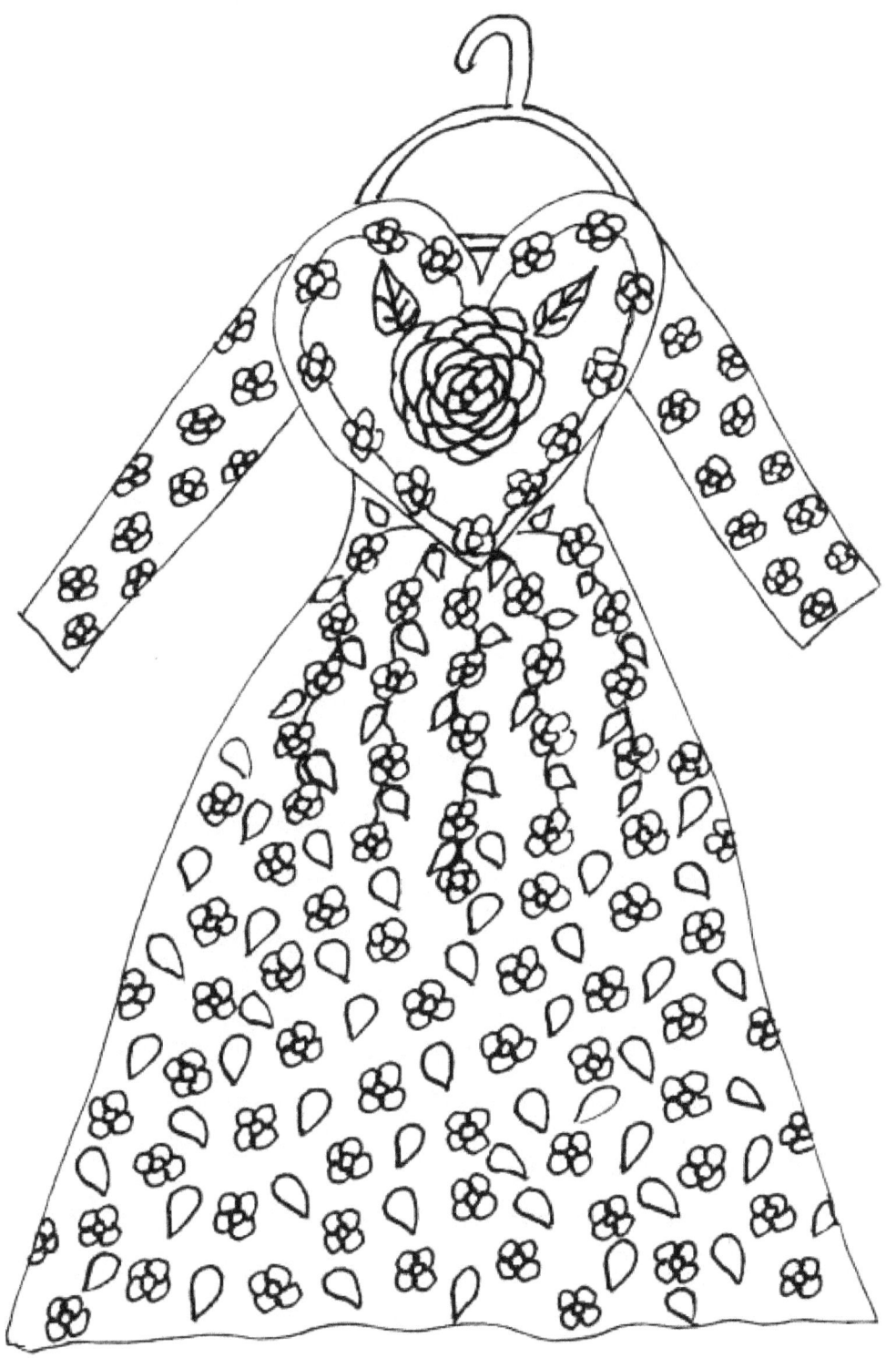

www.ingramcontent.com/pod-product-compliance
Lightning Source LLC
Chambersburg PA
CBHW060001230526
45472CB00008B/1899